T0149455

Seven Pillars

A Handbook for Existence

KEYTH GARCIA

SEVEN PILLARS
A HANDBOOK FOR EXISTENCE

iUniverse books may be ordered through booksellers or by contacting:

iUniverse
1663 Liberty Drive
Bloomington, IN 47403
www.iuniverse.com
1-800-Authors (1-800-288-4677)

ISBN: 978-1-5320-3239-4 (sc)
ISBN: 978-1-5320-3238-7 (e)

Library of Congress Control Number: 2017918782

Print information available on the last page.

iUniverse rev. date: 03/06/2018

PREFACE

SEVEN PILLARS IS TO be the first book people pick up when they are curious about the spiritual path. It is based on an occult text called the Kybalion. Texts like these demand that one read between the lines to discern the real meaning. *Seven Pillars* is a manual that has been read between the lines for you. It brings you face-to-face with the core knowledge provided in any spiritual, occult, or esoteric text you may come across.

I went to San Francisco State University, and over the past eight years, I've been taken from culture to culture, book to book, and speaker to speaker. I've been searching for this elusive truth. Believe me when I say that the amount of information on "spirituality" is endless—literally endless. The amount of rabbit holes is never-ending.

However, in the summer of 2013, I came across the Kybalion. The Kybalion speaks of the hermetic philosophy, which itself is based off a mythical set of fifteen indestructible emerald tablets of debatable origin. The tablets themselves have enough interest behind them to fill books, and in fact have. This book, however, is simply to go over the seven principles that were taken from the emerald tablets and to distill them even further into something that the average modern-day person can make use of.

When I started reading the Kybalion, I realized something—it was the first text that covered every other body of work I had come across in my search for truth and knowledge. Not only that, but it was concise. It did not rely on any external reading or searching. It was a one-stop source for knowledge and wisdom. It was the foundation for any other area of work in the occult or esoteric sciences. Whether it be alchemy, yoga, meditation, shamanism, Taoism, or Wicca, even the philosophies of great individuals throughout the ages, this hermetic philosophy and its seven principles were everywhere.

The Kybalion, however, was written in 1912. A great deal has happened since then. Many great scientific discoveries and many great individuals have graced the world with their presence. And they have all, in their own way, added to the validity of the hermetic philosophy. They fit in so flawlessly with the teachings of the Kybalion that I have decided to modernize it and include new discoveries since the Kybalion's release.

If you are looking for the most concise body of information to start you on your path to enlightenment or if you've been studying for decades and would like to condense that information into one body of knowledge, *Seven Pillars* is for you. Welcome home.

INTRODUCTION

RESIDING SOMEWHERE HERE ON earth, there are believed to be over a dozen tablets made of an indestructible, emerald-colored material created from alchemical transmutation.

These tablets are said to have engraved passages written in an ancient Atlantean language, the characters of which are said to react to the thought waves and intentions of the reader, allowing for a more powerful and personalized experience than the translated text can offer.

The text itself contains compelling words of wisdom and insight on matters that are still extensively discussed today, such as life and death, what it means to be free, the passing of time, cause and effect, the existence of magic, and many more.

The tablets are understood to have been written by an individual known in legends as Thoth, the Atlantean. Thoth is said to have left Atlantis at the time of its destruction and resettled in Egypt where he helped the Egyptians develop into the powerful civilization that we knew them to be.

The translations of the emerald tablets of Thoth can still be found in today's corpus hermeticum as they offer a deeper and more meaningful understanding of the knowledge gained from the legendary (and centuries older) emerald tablet of Hermes. The emerald tablet of Hermes is considered the oldest existing literature on alchemical and metaphysical contemplation. It has been translated countless times by many individuals interested in the alchemical nature of life, including physicist Isaac Newton.

This philosophy is not a religion but can be found in every religious text throughout the world. It is a universal layout of the operating systems of existence.

In front of you now is access to the same ancient wisdom, put into words we can all make sense of.

Seemingly irrefutable and consistent synchronicities fill our everyday lives. The only problem is that we have not yet been taught how to listen, how to see. To listen is to be aware, and to be aware is to be constantly engaged with each of our senses, with the flow of life that pervades our immediate structure for existence.

Imagine a lion in motion, stalking a herd of antelope. All her senses are in tune. She is downwind so that her smell drifts up and away. Her paws slide in and out of tall grass, softly, undetectable, because any sound she makes will give her away. Her amber-colored eyes stare ahead, unwavering, in hopes that her pack may eat plenty tonight.

Notice how all of a lion's senses must be engaged for her to be a successful hunter. There is no extra brain space for distracting thoughts when your life is on the line and no room for error. She must focus only on the present moment and let the instincts of millions of years of evolution take care of the rest, and this is how we must proceed. We must be like this lion. We must be so involved with our senses that not a single thought is able to penetrate our world.

When was the last time you were so caught up with *right now*— the present moment pervading you so deeply—that you forgot you were actually you? Was it at the birth of a child? A near-death experience? During sex? The mysteries of the world lie in the present moment—in paying attention to the warmth of the sun hitting your face, the coolness of a breeze arching across your cheeks, the smell of freshly cut grass or musky, damp earth.

Our conscious minds are only able to compute a fraction of what the universe has to offer at all times, from intangible wavelengths of energy to the faces we see walking by us on the street. When people say that life happens *right* now, they mean *right* now, and it is in this space that magic calls home.

Would you like to learn how to create your own reality, become a master of your thoughts, and be your own guru? Would you like to develop your intuition, reveal your passions? Do you desire to find out who you truly are, raise your vibration, transmute any energy into any other?

If so, you need to understand that you cannot achieve any of these things unless you sacrifice yourself to your senses as deeply and as often as you can. Paradoxically, however, this cannot be taught, and I'm actually not here to teach you anything.

I am here to show you that more important than your answers are your questions—not only to open doors to new worlds but to show you how to build your own doors with your own custom, boundless worlds inside. I'm here to show you how to construct a reality as easily and beautifully as an architect constructs a cathedral.

I'm here to show you that there are secrets in this world that are far more audacious than our imaginations currently allow us to process. I'm here to pose questions and reveal riddles that force your mind to wrap around itself in anguish because its foundations are shattered. I'm here to offer you seven fundamental laws of the universe that will make you question your current reality and everything in it.

You're about to embark upon a journey of wonders and beautiful mysteries. I must warn you, however. These types of things are best not to start if you do not intend to finish. This is not for those of you who wish to keep your cultural sanity, or those of you who are perfectly content with your current reality. If so, you better stop reading now. For the rest of you, welcome home.

Again, once you start, it is best to finish. Ready? Let's begin.

CHAPTER 1

The Substantial Reality—The All

When the ears of the student are ready to hear, then cometh the lips to fill them with Wisdom.

—*The Kybalion.*

WE BEGIN WITH THE ALL.

I do not mean for the introduction of this chapter to come off religious. I am not masking this philosophy as a new-age doctrine. Instead, I wish to show you natural laws of the world and of this universe, so that you may begin to see the patterns of things.

Learning to see patterns is nearly the same as being able to see the future. We use the known to predict the unknown and therefore increase our chances of creating worlds that are more in line with our desires, instead of methodical notions imposed upon our subconscious by forces outside of ourselves. I want to teach you about the mechanics of life and more importantly, the mechanics of yourself. We will soon see that both are one and the same.

I speak in terms of a substantial reality—a reality from which all things that we experience manifest. Outwardly, we see a world constantly changing—growing, dying, growing, dying, ad infinitum. This tells us there must be some internal mechanism—a framework for the known universe—from which all this change comes.

The substantial reality that we speak of must not be changing in itself, however. It must be constant, a rock from which we build all our principles. Otherwise, the patterns built into the known world would come apart, and chaos would soon after consume. This rock is The All, named as such not to be a deity, but it is simply the most all-encompassing word we can use for the topic.

To make it easier to comprehend, let's think about it from your perspective. When you look at the big picture of things, what do you see? Reality is defined as thus: the world or the state of things as they *actually* exist, as opposed to an idealistic or notional idea of them. What, then, is the reality of this world? What are the true mechanisms for which things outwardly manifest? I ask you, what is the one thing you can be absolutely sure of when you look out into the world, the one thing that never changes.

And because you are reading this book and are more than likely on a path of enlightenment, you would probably say, "I see that there is no one thing I can be *actually* sure of. Nothing out there in the world really *is*. Everything is just *becoming*. Once something hits its apex of growth, it begins its downward descent into nothingness, only to be brought back as something new. Change is really the only constant I see."

Beautiful! How incredibly observant you are, and you are absolutely correct. Change *is* the one thing we can be absolutely sure of.

Look at a pendulum and you see that things are swaying from one side of the pendulum to the other. There is no substantiality to anything. Change is the only constant. Everything—destruction, creation, inward and outward flow—is evolving from something else and resolving into something new. The thinking person, like yourself, would also deduct that because this law is as such, a law, it must be governed by *something*. It must have been set in something that is *not* changing, for this law itself remains constant.

We find that that *something* is actually the substantial reality, something that works outside this law of constant change: The All. And The All is, well, *all*. It encompasses and pervades everything. Nothing can be outside, before, nor after The All. It is the most basic, most substantial reality from which our universe and the infinite others operates. Everything is subject to it, but because of its infiniteness, it itself is subject to nothing. It is subject to no change. This is the substantial reality of existence.

Thinkers and philosophers throughout history have tried to give this substantial reality a name and have labeled it under various monotheistic, polytheistic, and even nature-based deities. Some have called it "the eternal and infinite energy." Scientists at one point tried to label it as matter. Its existence seems to be without need of proof, self-evident in that it is and isn't at the same time.

This is where the term "The All" comes from. As part of this philosophy, an understanding of The All will never be complete. To gaze upon and understand the infiniteness of The All is like Hamlet trying to understand Shakespeare's life story—impossible. The name "The All" is merely the best term to use to transfer as much meaning into tangible letters so we have an understanding of the capacity of this substantial reality.

We must also understand, however, that The All transcends names and definitions. We must accept that none but The All may understand its real and true inner workings—a divine paradox indeed.

This is where it gets tricky, if it hasn't already. The object of this book is not to get you to understand The All. The All is infinite; our minds are not. We already understand that our world operates based on change, and anyone trying to discern the inner nature of The All is doomed to a life of madness.

It is not our purpose to understand the inner nature of The All, at least not in this lifetime. It is only our job to understand those laws that emanate *from* The All, so that we may become players instead of pawns, not rising to fairy-tale heights by ways of wishy-washy magic but by using one law against the other, to rise ever higher within the planes of existence.

Furthermore, we must refrain from ascribing the qualities we find ourselves dealing with unto The All. All personalities, aesthetics, and characteristics that pertain to us do not fit The All, especially lowly characteristics such as jealousy, susceptibility to flattery and praise, and desire for offerings and worship. It is apparent why this philosophy at one point in time had to remain secret.

Now I'm going to drop some substance on you. I will break down what The All consists of as to give you some type of foothold—within reason—on how to proceed with this book. These guidelines will keep us from straying too far from the path of knowledge within the hermetic philosophy.

This is to ascertain the substantiality of The All without attempting to lift too much of the veil of the unknowable. Understand these three things as taken from the hermetic philosophy:

1. The All must be *all that really is*. There cannot be anything existing outside of The All, less The All, would not actually be, The All. Easy enough? On to part two.

2. The All must be infinite—infinite because there is nothing else to act upon it in which to actually limit it. In other words, nothing can define, confine, bound, or limit it. It also must be timeless, eternal. If it had a beginning, it must have come from something else, which would make it *not* The All. It also may not have an end, for there must be something outside The All in which to end it, and therefore something else to start up again, for there can never be non-experience. For these same reasons, it must be infinite in space and infinite in power. For there to be a limit in any way upon The All would suggest that there is something that is not a part of The All to act upon it. Since there is nothing outside of The All—The All being everywhere—there is nothing with which to limit it. It is subject to no other power, because there is no other power.

3. The All must be immutable. It must not be subject to change from its real nature. If it was subject to change, then it would *not* be the substantial reality, and therefore it would not be The All. There is nothing to act changes upon it and nothing that it could change into, for there is nothing outside The All. There is nothing to add to it or diminish it. Therefore its size—infinite—must also be constant. It must have always been just as it is at this moment. There is a saying in the Kybalion (the hermetic philosophy) that goes, "Nothing can rise higher than its own source." It took

me several reads to figure out exactly what this means, but alas, I've done it. Since I'm better at making analogies than the ancient text, I'll make sure it's comprehensible the first time around:

The simple version (according to physics): Hold a fifty-pound ball to your nose from a rope swing. Let it go so that it swings away from you. Now, as the fifty-pound ball comes screaming back toward your face, don't move, because the ball "cannot rise higher than its source." It will not hit you.

This is how we determine what The All is.

The All cannot be said to be matter. Why? Because again, nothing can rise higher than its own source. All around us we see life and mind (consciousness), yet we do not see life and mind in matter, so how can something greater than matter (life and mind) come from it? It can't. Nothing can manifest in an effect that first didn't originate within the cause. This may be a bit crude, but a dog cannot come from a cat.

Though matter has already been stripped of its previous title, scientists now say that matter is merely slowed down energy, energy brought to a standstill in order to manifest as a certain object. In other words, it is now known that matter is actually energy. It only took science about four thousand years to catch up with this one.

Now, you might guess that The All is energy. You're getting warmer. But energy, in terms of how we use the word today, still doesn't match. Energy today is mere mechanics, part of an equation, a stepping stone to get to something else. It also contains more than itself: life and mind, or consciousness. Remember, you and I are of life and mind, and energy, according to today's definitions, is by no means life and mind. For the reasons stated above, energy also cannot be The All. If energy and force, as we call it today, do not contain consciousness, and you and I are here using our minds, then no, The All cannot be merely energy. For within the effect must lie a piece of the cause. Something cannot rise higher than its source.

The Kybalion lists one possibility: that The All is life and mind. Again, we can't ascribe that it is exactly life and mind, for to put a label on The All as if to understand its inner nature would be like trying to define the infinite by the finite, which is inherently impossible. However, if life and mind is the highest manifestation of our universe, it must be a basis for The All to operate. Like with most things in life, the answer is both yes and no. The All is an infinite living mind, known by the ancients as *spirit*.

CHAPTER 2

The Law of Mentalism

THE AIM OF THIS chapter is to describe how The All uses the mind to create and that The All does in fact use the mind to create. Topics, discussions, and laws will be presented from a fundamental point of view that The All operates strictly out of the mind. As to be so bold, I will describe to you what life is—not the meaning of life, but its nature.

It begins with spirit. Spirit is an all living mind that pervades existence and rests gracefully across all philosophies of human kind. It is where the richness and vastness of creation begins. The law of attraction, mental creation, or the law of vibration are touched far too often and explained far too little. All seven of the basic hermetic laws are only capable with the understanding of the mental creation process.

Follow closely, and I will explain how infinity is possible, how we can tap into the universal laws of The All and its operating systems. We will enter our lives as magicians from here on out, but first things first. Let's discuss the universe. Within new age thought and spirituality, much of the terminology and paradigms are that the universe is The All.

The universe is not The All.

Due to the nature of The All, which we have already gone over, this cannot be. We see constant change within the universe and of the universe itself. Therefore, the universe cannot be The All, for there is nothing outside The All in which to instigate change. Remember, The All operates as the substantiality of existence. Thus it is the absolute truth and therefore must be unchanging.

This we have to accept.

If the universe is not The All, it must be an illusion of The All—or nothing—one would think. Yes and no, only this does not give us much understanding of what the universe actually is.

What is the universe, if not The All? Some philosophers have postulated that The All, or their interpretation of The All, divided itself or in some way replicated itself in order to create that which we see today. We know this to be false, since there is nothing outside The All to act upon its division. In other words, we cannot divide something in half without something to act as the divider.

There is a movement in New Age spirituality. Knowing that The All is truly The All, and us being an extension of The All, people shout, "*I am God,*" to the "amusement of the masses and sorrow of the sages." An infinitely modest analogy would be an ion exclaiming, "*I am man.*"

This might be a bit ground shaking to hear in today's spiritual practices, but we are not The All or God, or whichever name we choose to call it. We are no more God than Hamlet is Shakespeare.

So if The All didn't replicate itself or otherwise fragment itself into what we see today, how did the universe and life come about?

Let's incorporate a beautiful little law called the law of correspondence, one of my favorite hermetic axioms, which will be thoroughly explained in its own chapter later. This law dictates that anything that happens on a celestial level (in this case The All) must also happen at the corpuscle level (in this case everything else). We also see it written in the Bible as thus: as above, so below.

It means that we can figure out how the universe was created without The All physically dividing, reproducing, replicating, or any other means of fragmenting itself. We do this by seeing how the same process can be done here on earth with human consciousness. The reason we can do this lies in the definition of the law of correspondence: the act of creation on our plane of existence must by correspondence also be the same mechanism on the celestial level—as above, so below.

Let it be known that the path we are about to walk via the law of correspondence is the same path for any and all situations. This is the key to gaining wisdom about the unknown universe by the known.

Let's begin. What are some ways in which humanity creates?

1. Let's use the example of building a house. In what ways can we do this? You need a plethora of tools, right? Tools are things outside of yourself, however. We know that there is

nothing that exists outside of The All. Therefore, this first example is null. If there were something outside of The All, The All would not be The All. Easy enough—on to the next. How else does humanity create?

2. Procreation? Yes. This won't suffice, however. To procreate requires a multiplication of the self, and The All cannot multiply itself or transfer part of itself to something else, for where outside The All would it transfer? And what else is there to multiply with? After all, to add or subtract to The All is nonsensical. The All is as it has ever been and ever will be. It is unchanging in nature, for it is the absolute substantial reality. Therefore, procreation will also fall short of a satisfying answer based on the axioms of The All. What else is there, then? If not using tools nor procreation to create, how else do humans create? We grab from behind the veil.

3. Humanity uses mind. It uses mental creation processes to create limitless and boundless worlds without using any outside tools or reproducing itself. The All creates universes with mind. Just as we are able to create with mind, so does The All. Success! We have just aced our first quiz in self-mastery via the law of correspondence. The only difference is that we create with a finite mind, while The All creates with a limitless one. The process is the same, but the degree of difference is infinite. This tiny but infinitely important finding must be your takeaway for now—that the universe, and everything contained within it, is within the mental creation of The All.

My friends, we exist within a thought, within a dream.

Architects of Reality

You put water into a cup, it becomes the cup. You put
water into a teapot, it becomes the teapot. Water can
flow, or it can crash. Be water, my friend.

—B. Lee

This principle is very clear and very relevant, and absolutely nothing about it is new, especially within the new age movement. It states that The All, which is the meme of existence, the underlying foundation from which everything outwardly manifests, is the substantial reality in which everything arises.

The All is the phenomenon of life. Energy, matter—it all arises from spirit. It all arises from The All, which itself is indefinable, indescribable but can to the best of our humbled enterprises be called by us as a universal living mind.

This law also describes that everything we experience in our existence is happening within the mind of the all. All lifetimes and experiences, every thought and idea, every nebulae and black hole, are happening within the mind of The All. With this principle in place, we are allowed the psychic phenomenon that sits so readily within the public eye. Without the understanding of the mental universe, all such phenomena are undefinable and continue to defy scientific scrutiny.

The principle of mentalism is arguably one of the most substantial laws within the hermetic philosophy. With it, students may begin to use thought consciously and with focus.

By understanding this first law, we become active participants within our realities. Most importantly, understanding this principle allows for a much more thorough understanding of energy, power, and matter. We begin to understand that these things fall subordinate to the mastery of mind. It is claimed by one of the great masters of the hermetic teachings that this principle is the master key, and without it, mastery is impossible. As a result, the student knocks in vain at the many doors of the temples.

Now, I have basically covered the bird that sits at the tip of the iceberg as far as mentalism goes, but it's enough to take us into our first paradigm-destroying concept. Congratulations, you made it!

Circumstances Don't Matter; Only States of Being Matter

Transmutation used to be a word that described changing one metal into another. Usually it was lead into gold. However, this is not necessarily what alchemy is about. What is meant to be transmuted is one frame of mind to the next, one mental vibration to another—the heaviness of lead to the lightness of gold.

The reason why the principle of mentalism is so substantial is because everything begins within the mind. Remember, according to the law of mentalism, all universes exists within the mind of The All. Us being extensions of that creative process, and of The All, means we must also operate on the same concept—as above, so below.

This is where state of being comes into play. Every day we come across an infinite amount of various circumstances that are both small and large, good and bad, right and wrong depending upon our personal view and vantage point.

Normally, we let it dictate us. We use excuses as to why we are not where we want to be. We put our well-being in the hands of forces beyond our control. We say things like, "I am not successful because I was not given stature," or "I am not happy because these events must first take place."

You see, if we want to be creators of our realities, we must actually be creators. We must create from nothing. An architect does not say he cannot build on a particular piece of land because it is uneven. He simply does what is necessary to even the land and builds what he came there to build.

"To hell with circumstances. I create my own opportunities," said the ever-elucidating martial artist Bruce Lee. With what did Lee use to formulate this notion of himself as a creator?

His mind.

He made a clear decision. He formed a conclusion of the world that made him a creator and polarized himself firmly in it. From here he proceeded.

You see, the interesting thing about universal truths is that you don't really have to know them to use them. These laws operate all around us, and we can either be dictated by them or use them to control our lives and the world around us. We must be open to all possibilities because all possibilities are possible.

Now, I'm not saying we must accept all happenings. I'm saying we must not be surprised when they do happen. We must be aware of our mind-sets and be careful not to solidify them. We must be formless with our interpretation of reality—like water—because reality is constantly changing and is itself formless.

Circumstances will never be exactly how we need them to be, and to wait for that to happen is to let the outside world dictate your well-being. To wait for the world to be perfect is to wait an awfully long time, and that is not what we are here for.

How to Create from Mind

It is easy.

Step one: play. Turn everything into a game. Turn everything into something that moves you.

Unfortunately, culture teaches us that if you are having too much fun, you are somehow not working hard enough. Play and work are always separated. We even have phrases like "all work and no play," in our culture. Words program the mind, and sayings like this teach us that these two things are not the same.

I say to hell with culture.

Terence Mckenna, who was an American ethnobotanist, mystic, psychonaut, lecturer, author, and advocate for the responsible use of naturally occurring psychedelic plants, had it right when he said culture is not our friend. Remember, we are referencing the law of mentalism, which says that everything begins with the mind.

It says creation begins in the mind.

Why not use our minds to create a paradigm in which we are just as successful with getting things done while still enjoying ourselves while we do it? Why not allow play to be a part of our work instead of separating it? Our lives are torn enough as it is. Why make it more difficult on ourselves?

Step two: Our emotions have physical, measurable wavelengths, and I could not care less if science has proved it or not. I would still believe it. Why? Because I know how quickly the atmosphere of a room can change when someone loses his or her mind in anger. I feel its restrictions. The tension of anger is quite literally palpable, and for me, that is enough proof that emotions have real, measurable effects on the physical world.

With that said, the energy we bring into any situation will directly influence the energy flow within that encounter. This is why play is such a substantial and overwhelmingly useful tool when entertaining the principle of mental creation.

Think about what we associate with the word *play*. According to a thesaurus, it is associated with words like *lighthearted, buoyant, expansive, high-spirited,* and *sprightly* (I included this last one for my faery folk). What do all these words have in common? Lighthearted, buoyant, and high-spirited all imply a sense of weightlessness, of ease. These words, more or less, lift us up.

Remember, we are creating with our minds. If our minds are programmed to think that the word *play* consists of words like these, what would that do to any situation we introduce play to? The law of correspondence says that the situation will be weightless, that it will progress with more ease. It will follow the word *play*.

It is impossible to play and not have fun. There is no way we can have these synonyms of the word *play* built into our vocabulary, yet apply them to a situation and they have a different effect on the outcome or circumstance. An effect will always contain within it fragments of the cause. Words are incredibly powerful because each word contains a definition that our minds use to create reality. Words heavily influence the mind, and the mind is responsible for the generation of worlds.

The energy you bring into any given situation will in turn have a real and palpable effect on that situation. Through association and the law of correspondence, we now understand the expansive, uplifting, and lighthearted energy of the word *play* and can use it to shape our experiences.

Play long enough, and after a while you will start to notice some truly incredible things. Your outside world will begin to mirror your inside world. The space you have created within yourself will reverberate back out into the world and begin to fill it with circumstances that fit this new paradigm of thought.

This is how the law of attraction works. You are what you think. In the movie *Inception*, Leonardo DiCaprio's character explains that the architects of the dream world create the framework, and then the individual fills the dream with his or her own experiences. Thus, your dream world is only going to be as good as the framework you lay out for it. If you have a subpar framework for your dreams, then your dreams will be unfavorable. If you have a subpar mental framework for your life, your life will be unfavorable.

Therefore, stay aware in every situation you encounter. Be a witness to your emotions and reactions. Awareness of your emotions, at any given point, is an indication of whether your thoughts are in check.

This constant state of what I call "awareness and shift, awareness and shift, awareness and shift," will eventually tell the universe, "these are the circumstances that I desire." You begin to shift, and the universe acts accordingly. Watch the synchronicities flow.

CHAPTER 3

Law of Correspondence

As above, so below; as below, so above.

—*The Kybalion*

Now, LET's DIVE INTO the law of correspondence once and for all. Laws are only binding when we do not know how to use them properly. We apply law against law to rise above certain planes of existence and further our evolutionary processes. My grandfather used to always say, "You have to know the rules before you can break them." If we truly understand the meaning and implications of this law, we can obtain massive breakthroughs within our lives. It is a skeleton key that unlocks doors to understanding the universe and more importantly, the self.

There is a correspondence between all things on every plane of existence: the mental, physical, and spiritual planes. The Hermetic axiom says, "As above, so below; as below, so above." Keep this thought in mind and you will grasp concepts of unknown worlds by studying the known.

Geometry is the tool astronomers use to calculate the mass of an invisible black hole thousands of light-years away while seated comfortably in their observatories. A knowledge of the principle of correspondence enables a person to reason intelligently from the known to the unknown by studying the monad he learns of the archangel.

As stated in the previous chapter, the law of correspondence says that anything found within the microcosmic level is found on the macrocosmic level, so let's look at how it operates in the grand scale of the universe. Scientists say the universe is roughly 156 billion light years wide, with clusters of giant groups of galaxies. This says the universe is mostly space.

If the universe as a whole is mostly space, by the law of correspondence, so must everything else be within the universe— as above, so below. Now let's go below and shrink down to our own galaxy. Epic amounts of light would make one think that a galaxy is mostly filled. It is not. It is made of only a handful of celestial bodies. It is also mostly space.

Shrink down further to our solar system. The sun is 93 million miles away from us, with only eight planets orbiting it, covering hundreds of millions of miles of orbit. It's like a golf ball orbiting a basketball court. Again, mostly space.

Let's shrink down even smaller, to the human body. We would think the body is dense, right? It is so dense that, with enough practice, our hands could cut a brick in half or the pressure of our solid fingers can play keys on a piano. We are very solid, indeed. It turns out that our bodies and the atoms we consist of are also mostly space.

Quantum scientists have found that if the nucleus of an atom were the size of a basketball, the orbiting electrons—which define the outer limits of the atom—would be something like twenty miles away. That's 99.999 percent space! A basketball is about a foot across, and for its outer edge to be twenty miles away means that for twenty miles, there is nothing but space.

All atoms are this way, which means once it touches up against another atom, that other wall is also twenty miles away from its nucleus. That's a full forty miles of space between two basketballs. These forty miles of space make up all of our physical reality.

Forty miles of space make up the atoms of the sun, water molecules, the ocean, your hand, a feather. Forty miles of space make up everything solid within the universe. This is what I mean when I say that from nothing comes everything. Nothingness gives birth to the something.

The law of correspondence creates a web of interconnectedness so complex it's difficult to even put into perspective, yet I will try. The All is infinite, right? It is infinite in that it contains everything and there is nothing outside of it. All ideas, happenings, events, possibilities, and lifetimes have happened within The All, which consists mostly of space. That must mean that from space, or nothingness, comes infinity and all possibilities.

Since this is one of the principal operating systems of The All, everything within The All must operate in this same manner. This means we can apply it to everything. It is the shape of the nothing that gives definition to the something. The reason the universe is infinitely possible is because it comes from something that can give shape to anything. It is made of nothing but pure potential, and that pure potential is the nothingness that contains everything.

Nothingness is not what we think it is. It isn't the absence of something. It is more like the nothing that holds the entirety of all celestial bodies. Nothingness is simply unsolidified potential capable of taking on any form when instigated by consciousness. It's the definition of everything. It gives "space" to beauty and form to creation.

It allows a thing to shine and thrive and individualize into newer and more complex patterns than before. Artists use this all the time when creating. They call it negative space. The late American jazz musician Miles Davis said, "Music is the space between the notes. It's not the notes you play, it's the notes you don't play." Wolfgang Amadeus Mozart said the same thing: "The music is not in the notes, but in the silence between," and so did the composer of "Clair de Lune," Claude Debussy: "Music is the space between the notes."

Beautiful, is it not?

I understand that all of this may sound too much like fantasy— beautifully word-smithed and carefully crafted soliloquies from a far too introspective mind—and I agree, this is probably true. However, the one incredible thing about this law is that if it happens on any plane of existence—even on the philosophical and universal level—it must also happen everywhere else, even in the physical and mental levels. Now that science has caught up with these age-old teachings, what does it have to say about the concept that from nothing comes all?

Using the unified field theory, quantum physicists have determined that there is a universal field of energy that is pure potential. A revelation in quantum physics speaks of the potential within electrons. It is called the double-slit theory. The conclusion of the experiment was that protons can be both solid and waveform at the same exact time.

This means they can be nothing and something simultaneously. It is important to know that these electrons make up everything in the universe. Can you imagine that? That everything in the universe is made of particles that are both something and nothing at the same time? We are talking pure potential.

My friends, you are made, literally, of pure potential.

How to Win Any Argument

Now, let's use the law of correspondence in practicality. We'll take it into the world of interpersonal communications. Have you ever wanted to learn how to easily communicate your thoughts and views without running in wild, heated circles? In other words, would you like to learn how to navigate any argument with ease?

This is how you do it: Listen to what the other person is saying. If you want to be successful in dealing with people, whether it's your spouse, a coworker, a parent, a child, students, or teachers, you have to listen to what they are saying. Otherwise, you miss everything.

The law of correspondence says anything that happens without, happens within, and anything that happens within, happens without. Say your boss looks at you and says, "It's a dog-eat-dog world. Life will chew you up and spit you out if you let it."

Is that so? Yes, of course. To him or her, it's the absolute truth. Remember, our definitions of the world are based solely on our experiences within it. After all, we cannot define the world by things that have not happened to us and by experiences we have not yet lived. It wouldn't make any sense. It would be like me trying to give advice to a woman on how to be a woman. I have no place in that world, so I have no right to speak. On being a man, however, I may comment as much as I like.

With that said, we cannot get into an argument on how the world is when our worlds are literally different. This is how we all live in varying realities in the same world. We all "are" and "are not" at the same time.

If someone starts crying because of the beauty of a falling leaf, we know that this person appreciates the beauty in the small things to the point of tears. We know that anything we do around this person will probably be met with appreciation and wonder.

If someone says, "Screw women. All they do is play games and manipulate," does that mean that all women do is play games and manipulate? Absolutely, but only to that person. Have you heard the phrase, "Those who live by the sword die by the sword"? People who play games and manipulate attract people who play games and manipulate. Our perceptions of the world define our world, and as a result, we attract that which we think into our lives. And if we don't attract it, we create it. So with that person who thinks women manipulate, he is actually creating that "truth" in his own world, true in his but none other. That's what I mean when I say he is "right." Right and wrong can very subjective, though.

Again, the secret to win any argument is to genuinely listen to the person you are talking to—to put yourself in his or her situation and fully understand where he or she is coming from and meet him or her halfway, because only then may you turn the conversation around.

This is how we use the law of correspondence to our advantage. It's how we become the chess player instead of being the chess piece. The game doesn't change, only our roles.

From here we learn to take control of our lives by controlling our states of being. It is great to know how to deal with what lies outside of us, but that is also all we can do, because by no means will we ever be able to completely control them. Too much is left up to variables outside our control.

All we can control is ourselves and our own perceptions of the world, which leads me to the most important part of this topic. The law of correspondence is most useful when we use it to figure out who we really are and how we operate, not others. Just like listening to others during an argument to see where they are coming from, we should do the same with ourselves.

Listen to the words you use and look at the paradigms you have created that define how the world operates. Remember, the conclusions you have come to are conclusions based solely off of your experiences and how you have interpreted them, meaning they are only absolutely true when it comes to you and only you.

This is where we take ultimate control over our lives. Whatever you find yourself running into over and over again is based on the conclusions you have made about the world. In order to shift into something we desire to become, we must first change our ideas and concepts of the outside world. We must drop our biases for something a bit more wholesome.

How do we do that? Sometimes life happens, and it takes a toll on our well-being since we are ultimately influenced by things outside of our control. This is the way it must be, however. The outside world absolutely influences the inside world, but it's the inside world we have control over.

If we are able to stay at peace with what is happening on the outside, we maintain peace on the inside. After all, it is said that peace does not mean to be in a place with no noise, trouble, or hard work. It means to be in the midst of those things and still be calm in your heart, mind, and soul.

It is always better to light a match than to curse the darkness. This way, we begin happening to the world instead of the world happening to us. We must change the inside, and the outside changes with it. As above, so below.

I have now explained the theoretical part of the law of correspondence, and it is time to look at some practical ways of achieving the way of being I have described above. What are some necessary steps we must take to reach an observer mind-set?

1. Take a sincere look at your current reality—your career, finances, relationships, and health. Look at these things and ask yourself which inner thoughts are being transposed to the outside. What conclusions have you come to that are not serving you anymore? Remember, your experiences are yours. They are not bad or good; they just are. They served their purpose for the time, but now it is time to grow. It is time to evolve and to learn new lessons from new experiences. Witness where the paradigms of your world come from, and learn from them. Once you do this, you'll be in a position to make decisions that move you into a

direction that is more in tune with where you really want to be. The best way to do this is to proceed without judgment on yourself, because underneath it all, you are made of love and light. You've only acted to gain as much happiness as you could, just like the rest of us. We are all in this together. Follow love, follow passion and excitement, smile, laugh, and always remember that you are made up of subatomic particles with infinite potential. Every part of you screams, "I can be anything!" First, look at who you are now. Accept, let go, and trust the bigger part of you and let it out.

2. Take responsibility! I know, I hate this word too, or at least I used to, back when I wasn't as good at seeing things for what they really are. Then I realized responsibility merely means your ability to respond—no more, no less. Your mind is an incredibly powerful mechanism. We project into the universal field with our minds, and therefore we project our realities. When we tell the universal field that we are responsible for our lives and what goes on in them— both good and bad—we tell the universe that we wish to be creators. We say, "These things are happening because of me. Therefore, it is I who have the power to change them." We tell the universe that we wish to be sentient beings who dictate the circumstances of our lives. If we put blame on outside influences, for either good or bad, we also put power into outside influences. Therefore, we are at the mercy of outside happenings, pawns instead of players. So take responsibility.

3. Last, focus. When all the shenanigans have passed, we can continue forward. Let bygones be bygones, say thank you for the experiences, the lessons, and move on with your life. I live in Southern California, where we are tormented with droughts lasting tens of years. We pump water to

feed people and agricultural lands from hundreds of miles away. We have signs that say, "Where water flows, food grows." Let's bring in the law of correspondence here and say, "Where attention flows, life grows." Scientists have reworded their ideas of matter to call it an interruption in energy waves. In other words, it is energy that has slowed down and condensed into matter. You may use your focus to do the same thing. Let your focus and attention be only on what benefits you. Consciously slow down your mind to the present moment so reality may condense around you. If something bothers you, do not complain, do not judge, for you are only putting energy into that thing which you do not like. Where water flows, food grows. The less your focus can be divided, the better you will be at creating realities that make sense to you. Focus on creating the good, not condemning the bad.

CHAPTER 4

Law of Vibration

*If you want to find the secrets of the universe, think in
terms of energy, frequency and vibration*

—*Nikola Tesla*

EVERYTHING IN THE UNIVERSE is in motion—oscillating,
moving, circling. Look closely at our atoms, and you see the circling
movement of electrons. Zoom out and you see the moon orbiting
the earth, the earth orbiting the sun, the sun orbiting the center of
the galaxy, and as far as we know, the center of the galaxy circling
the center of a clusters of galaxies, ad infinitum.

However, it doesn't stop with just material things. States of being,
emotions, and ideas are also in constant motion. Everything has
varying frequencies of vibration, and it is this difference in vibration
that separates one "thing" from another.

Pure spirit, or The All, is to be seen as an infinitely high vibrational
state. So high, in fact, that it might be seen as standing still,
like a quickly rotating wheel. From one pole to the other—like

happiness to sadness—there exists an infinite number of different frequencies, all coexisting at different states of vibration. They appear as matter, thoughts, emotions, electricity, magnetism, and every other phenomenon we see in the world.

Ancient hermetists speak of using this law to manipulate matter as well as mental states of being. This chapter will strictly focus on the latter, however, for I have not yet mastered the law enough to create my own apple tree out of thin air.

In order to use the law of vibration effectively, we must understand that the mental states in which we operate are literally tangible and palpable. Just like material objects have their degree of vibration—from orbiting electrons to orbiting galaxies—so do mental states.

Emotional vibrations range from low frequencies to high frequencies. When you enjoy life and everything seems to go your way, your vibration is higher. When they don't go your way, it's lower.

It's almost like being in love. You know that feeling of lightness and a soaring confidence? That's the feeling you get when your emotions are adding voltage and power to each and every one of your cells, which is exactly what happens when you're in love.

When you're negative and depressed, however, you feel sluggish and tired, which is why we use words like feeling *heavy, low,* and *down.*

Isn't it funny how the words we use match the location of our frequencies?

Your emotional vibrations are giving your body a slower, lower vibration when you are not well. This is not speaking metaphorically. It is scientifically measurable. Dr. Candace Pert, among many others, is a renowned neuroscientist who spent her life researching brain waves and their influence on the body.

With an understanding of this, we can bring awareness to our thoughts and monitor them closely. Emotions like joy, gratitude, and love register as much-higher frequencies, while emotions like fear, hate, and envy register as low frequencies.

Our emotions literally influence our physical reality.

A famous experiment by scientist Dr. Masaru Emoto of Japan was based on programming the structure of water molecules with thought.

During the experiment, Dr. Emoto subjected water to various ideas and concepts. Some held low frequencies like fear, hate, and jealousy, and others held high frequencies like love, peace, and truth. He then froze the water and looked at the water molecules under a microscope. He found that the high frequency–charged water molecules showed absolute beautiful symmetry, while the low frequency–charged water molecules lacked symmetry altogether.

The more we operate in certain states of consciousness, the more we broadcast that frequency out into the world. This is how the law of attraction works.

Resonance is defined by science as the reinforcement or prolongation of sound by reflection from a surface or by the synchronous vibration of a neighboring object. This means two things of the same frequency will always vibrate together as long as one vibrates.

The best example of this is found in musical instruments. If you play an E note on a violin, all other E notes on all violins in the same room will begin to vibrate to that original violin without being plucked themselves.

The frequencies of the world mirror this idea of resonance. We project a certain wavelength, throwing light or darkness out into the world in every direction, like the sun. These invisible waves strike anything and everything—your own personal magic feelers extending from your heart and out into the universe. Like attracts like, so when a wave strikes something that matches itself—another thought pattern, a bird, a human, a rock, it doesn't matter—these intelligent feelers seek out their counterparts like lovers in the night.

When your frequency strikes something in tune with itself, its counterpart begins to vibrate—an energetic dance on a subatomic level—and you have successfully started the attraction process. Hold on to that desired broadcast for long enough, and watch the other side come to life. This happens whether you're consciously aware of it.

Congruent frequencies will always evoke each other, whether it be two instruments resonating with each other or two different emotions self-inspiring. If you can identify the frequency broadcasted, you should be able to figure out what type of circumstance that frequency will manifest.

When it comes to evoking these magical experiences, our subconscious minds are in control, much more so than our conscious minds. Our subconscious minds, like the water from Dr.

Emoto's experiments, can be programmed by both circumstances and our conscious efforts. When our subconscious minds have been programmed, it takes on that form, like water, and radiates that energy back out into the world.

This is the important part to remember. We have to be constantly aware of how we program our subconscious minds, because just like water, they will take that shape and reverberate it back out into the universe.

The vibrations that come out of your heart and mind stimulate your surrounding area, just like the sound of strings on a guitar stimulate you to dance, and we want the world to dance to our song.

When we play music with someone else, or play along to a song, you can only create harmony when you play notes that lie within the musical scale of that same song. If I am playing Pachelbel's famous "Canon in D" and someone else wants to play along with me, he or she must also be playing in the key of D. Otherwise, the notes will clash. No matter how beautifully the other artist is playing, the two of us will sound terrible together.

Now, in terms of resonance, you're only going to dance to the music that is harmonious and literally resonating with your body. Just like the violin strings, you begin to vibrate back to the music. You begin to dance. Matching frequencies mean we evoke circumstances in our lives. It means we have the world dance to our song. We set the tempo, and we set the framework.

This is why it is so important to constantly monitor our thoughts. You're trying to evoke a reaction from the things you desire in the world that you would otherwise never come into direct contact with. This is where we can program our subconscious minds with a new construct for reality. When we do this, we allow a 24–7 broadcast of frequencies that are more in harmony with what we really want out of life. That's why it is so important to be clear about your intentions and visions. It gives the world a chance to dance to your song. The clearer the image is in your mind, the clearer its ethereal counterpart begins to resonate with it.

It's not about what's "good" or what's "bad." The universe and our world do not operate on these principles. They operate on vibration. Does the vibration match? Yes. Then we have harmony and resonance and therefore attraction and evocation of the two objects. What if the vibrations don't match? We get turbulence similar to two streams trying to flow into each other. We get no harmony and no attraction.

If only we could see with our eyes the invisible frequencies from our thoughts and actions reverberate out into open space and light up like fireworks in the sky as they strike something of similar cause. There are sparks of red tearing across the sky when our anger meets someone else's, or streaks of blue-green magenta when we pass a soulmate.

It would be an interesting world if we could see what our hearts see, wouldn't it? Maybe we can. Maybe that's why yogis, shamans, and healers try so desperately to connect us to our internal worlds, because to truly see within is to truly see without. Perhaps when we understand the language of the heart, we can begin to navigate this plane with a much better idea of the subtleties that billow and bounce from human to human, thought to thought.

I don't know, but it keeps me up at night.

The Human Body Is a Magnet

Would you like to attract certain experiences into your life? How about walk down the street and accidentally bump into your soulmate, spill your coffee, and have your fairy-tale novel begin? Maybe you want to stumble upon the one true ring so you can start your fantasy dream instead?

No problem. I will tell you how.

Magnets.

According to the World Health Organization, electric fields are created by differences in voltage: the higher the voltage, the stronger the resultant field will be. Magnetic fields are created when electric current flows: the greater the current, the stronger the magnetic field.

In other words, where there is an electrical current, there is a magnetic field: an electromagnetic field.

The study of neuropsychology shows that within the human brain and the entire nervous system, neurons communicate with each other through synapses via nerve impulses. Nerve impulses are waves of electrical activity that pass from one neuron to the other through the synapse. These electrical impulses carry information much in the same way electrical activity carries music information through wires into your headphones.

The brain alone contains around 100 billion neurons, each neuron constantly sending out nerve impulses as they communicate with each other. The amount of electrical activity going on in the human body is phenomenal. Remember, where electricity moves, there is an electromagnetic current. Humans are magnets.

This is what the *Journal of Theoretics* has to say about humans and their electromagnetic fields:

> The electric charges coursing through the human brain are measurable by means of an electroencephalogram. Humans thus have an electromagnetic (EM) energy field. As a result, the human body could act as an aerial that has the potential for simultaneous transmission and reception of energy with its environment … Our very physical bodies could be aerials that could simultaneously transmit EM energy to and receive EM energy from our physical environment, including to and from other people; and that this energy does indeed influence us as both emotions and thoughts.

Studies show that we are able to pick up on other people's electromagnetic fields through touch, or even by being in the same proximity. The EM field has been shown to broadcast several feet away from the center of a person's heart.

While we are on the topic of the heart, this is what the Royal College of Psychologists has to say about the heart's magnetic field:

> Research has revealed that the heart communicates information to the brain and throughout the body via EM field interactions. The heart generates the body's most powerful and most extensive EM field. The heart's magnetic component is about 500 times stronger than the brain's magnetic field and can be detected several feet from the body. It was proposed that this heart field acts as a carrier wave for information that provides

a global synchronizing signal for the entire body. (McCraty, Bradly & Tomasino, 2004)

The researchers are basically stating that the heart may act as a synchronizing component, bringing the body into harmony to increase the rhythmic properties of bodily functions. They continue to describe heart field interactions between individuals:

> There is now evidence that a subtle yet influential electromagnetic or 'energetic' communication system operates just below our conscious awareness. Energetic interactions possibly contribute to the 'magnetic' attractions or repulsions that occur between individuals, and also affect social relationships. It was found that one person's brainwaves can synchronize to another person's heart.

Beautiful. Simply beautiful. The human body is such an extraordinary thing.

How to Increase Your Body's Magnetism to Attract What You Want

This is a theory of my own, and it is just that: a theory. Take what I say here with a grain of salt. This description should spark you to pursue your own creative rabbit holes. I will use the law of correspondence to demonstrate how we can make the human body a more efficient magnet based on the properties of regular magnets. Keep in mind that I speak of the human electromagnetic field drawing in subtle matching frequencies, not actual iron as you walk through town.

As stated earlier, to make a magnet, you must get an electrical current flowing through a metal. What we did not mention before was that a magnet's strength can be increased by introducing more electricity to the metal; up the electricity, and you up the electromagnetic field.

If I place an iron nail on top of paper clips, nothing happens. If I wrap copper wire around the iron nail and put it to the paper clips, still nothing happens. But when I add electricity to the wire, something our ancestors would have called "magic" happens. Attach the copper wire ends to a battery, and the nail lifts the paper clips from the table without coming into contact with them.

This is how an electromagnetic field is created. The iron nail is the metal, the battery provides the electric current, and the copper wire provides the road that the current travels on. The flow of electricity through the wire creates an electromagnetic field, turning the iron into a magnet.

Since humans have billions of neurons firing information in the form of electrical signals, we have a substantial amount of electric current. Therefore, we have our own substantial electromagnetic fields.

Not only do we have the electric current in the form of firing nerve cells, but we also have the central nervous system, which acts as the channel, just like the copper wire. But it doesn't end there. Within our blood, there is iron, which just so happens to have some of the most unique characteristics when it comes to magnetic materials.

Let me rephrase that: At the center of every blood cell is iron. Your blood is pumped throughout the body, and the point of origin and finish is at the center: the heart. This explains why the heart's electromagnetic field is so much stronger than the brain's. It is possible the human magnetic field is driven by iron circulating throughout the body, creating its own electromagnetic field.

Since electricity can be converted from one form to another, we can deduce that the iron in our blood can be energized by different means. This is why eating vibrant foods that are still alive is said to raise a person's vibration. A kale leaf is still undergoing photosynthesis even when it is not on the plant. Thus, it is still alive and vibrant as you eat it. It has a high frequency.

But the connection I want you to make isn't that vibrant thoughts or foods will raise your vibration. I want to get away from the pseudo-science and more into the realm of the natural mechanics of the body.

To raise your magnetism means you concentrate a higher frequency into your body. More importantly, in this case, it is into the iron in your blood.

Remember, the more energy we put into the metal, the stronger the magnetic field becomes. Vibrant foods and thoughts concentrate more energy into your body, which strengthens your electromagnetic field, which in turn increases your ability to energetically pull whatever you desire closer to you. This is the same way the earth's electromagnetic field pulls objects into its orbit. As above, so below. It doesn't end with foods and thoughts, though.

Many guided meditations I come across insist that I imagine cosmic energy pouring into my body, while releasing the heavy unwanted energies into the earth. Since we now scientifically know that thoughts have measurable effects on objects, what does that say about this particular meditation practice? Through it, we literally use our minds to funnel cosmic energy into the body to stimulate the cells, and more importantly, within the iron in our blood—again, further increasing the potency of our electromagnetic pull.

When you put two positive sides of a magnet together, they repel each other. This is because energy flows out of the positive side of a magnet. We can avoid this by polarizing ourselves to a desired outcome. Let me explain.

When you polarize yourself to a desired outcome—in a moment of fear or insecurity, for example—you create a paradigm in which to act. If I were to embody one of my favorite characters, Gandalf from J.R.R. Tolkien's work, I would have a designed character I could simply plug myself into. Whenever needed, I could ask myself, "What would Gandalf do?" then act accordingly. It sounds silly, but it works.

It works because when we polarize ourselves to something we desire, we give the energy a specific path to follow. It comes in from the bottom and exits through the top, just like a magnet.

To see this in action, imagine two people having a conversation about politics. In any healthy conversation there should be a rhythm of conversing. One talks, one listens. If both people are centered and receptive, the flow of the conversation is healthy. The energy flows out of one and into the other and is then reciprocated back into the speaker. Just like putting the positive end of a magnet to the negative of the opposite, it becomes much stronger than before.

On the contrary, if both people try to speak up over one another, it is the same as pushing the positive sides of two magnets together—they repel each other.

To increase the likelihood of attracting what you want in life, you must do two things. You must first see yourself walking magnet powered by a personal electromagnetic field, because you are. Second, you must become clear about who you are so the signal you broadcast is as well defined as the things you wish to attract.

When you are clear about your uniqueness, who you are and aren't, you create a stronger vibrational message. Your chances of attracting like-minded, like-spirited people and systems increase as you become more aware of your thoughts, habits, and nutrition. Use your imagination to further concentrate higher frequencies into your body. Meditation is just one of the ways to accomplish this.

We have been given the opportunity to play an incredible role here—to be ourselves, and to express and transpose our heart's beauty and love onto everything we come across. I don't believe we are here to label ourselves as painters, builders, or teachers. These are just outward manifestations of expressions. The common denominator is the avenue of interpretation and self-elucidation while using whatever medium we choose. We paint from our hearts, build from our dreams, and teach to convey firsthand experiences and messages, while deepening our own understanding of the world. I don't believe it matters how we choose to express ourselves, as long as it represents our truest selves. No, we are not painters, builders, or teachers. We are dreamers, lovers, and messengers.

How do we create our lives based on being true to ourselves, then? Simple. Through excitement and bliss. Our objective shouldn't be to become a firefighter but to save lives, not to be an astronaut but to explore the vastness of space, the wonders and beauty that lie within it.

The way we express ourselves should be the career goal in life. Excitement is the fuel that burns and ignites our path of expression. Without excitement and passion, what else drives us forward? Excitement is a vibratory experience. It's one of the most energetic, uplifting, and euphoric emotions that humans can experience. Remember, the more powerful the emotion, the stronger the frequency broadcasted, the more it affects the surrounding world, and the more it evokes.

What's interesting about following excitement instead of singling in on a specific profession is that it allows for flexibility to continually do what makes you happy. If at any particular moment, the most exciting thing for you to do is to go for a walk, then go for a walk. If you are called to drop everything you're doing and go watch the sunset, go do that. After all, beauty demands a witness, and she will properly thank you for it. When you follow the heart, you never know what ideas might come up on the way, or who you might run into who could help you on your journey.

This brings me to my next point.

Forget about the how. It is not our job to make sense of everything that is happening at every moment. It is only our job to express our true selves and to be excited about it. When we let expression and excitement dictate our lives, we allow the universal law of vibration to dictate the movement. We begin to attract the resources we need, the people we want, the situations and the encounters we desire. When we maintain a high vibrational state, communities will build themselves around us.

It's just like playing music. Vibrations resonate with each other. Either notes fit within a scale or they don't. Learn to play with the music of life. It is impossible for lower states of vibration to exist around us when we maintain a high vibration through active participation in our own mental stability.

I encourage you to let excitement be your guide because your experiences only ever really make sense in hindsight. We can only connect the dots when we look backward. To trust your passion and intuition is a courageous thing most people do not have the guts to do because of the risks that seem to come with it. However, we must not forget that there is no such thing as failure. First of all, failure only happens when you give up. Second, "failure" only means you're doing something new, that you are pushing the boundaries, and there's a certain type of beauty in novelty. It gets rid of the mundane and allows us to expand into areas in our lives that need work.

I understand that the idea may seem wishy-washy or like I'm advocating that abandoning your goals and purposes is a good idea. It might be confused with "shiny object syndrome" or the inability to stay committed to something. To be completely honest with you, they might be right. After all, I am no ascended master, nor do I claim to be. I am just like you, perfectly flaw-ridden and doing my best to not slip off the surface of the earth into the desolate darkness of space.

This, however, does not worry me because I also must express myself. I have a commitment to demand from my life nothing but pure, unadulterated excitement and excellence, and if I can't manage to fit my avenues of expression into modern paradigms for the way it *should* be done, then so be it. My goal is to live and love, to show others the compassion they deserve, and to be thankful for every beautiful moment this place has given me.

If you are afraid that you may have shiny object syndrome—like me—I have an easy fix for you. If it is our excitement that fuels synchronicities in the manifestation of wanted circumstances, then we must make sure that our definitions for excitement match those goals. In other words, you must evaluate your definitions of excitement, evaluate your intentions.

Are you really excited about something, or are you just playing the role so you can avoid something else? Does this thing, this excitement, really move you? Or have you altered your definitions of excitement to avoid doing that which is truly more representative of yourself and your goals?

For example, I used to sometimes justify drinking, partying, and everything that goes with it in terms of excitement. Of course it's exciting, but does poisoning my mind and body through excessive impulsive behaviors and waking up with a throbbing headache represent my goals? Does it represent my truth in expressing myself, and can it realistically be used as an example of the law of vibration to attract that which I truly want in life? Absolutely not.

Then how can I use the vibrational state of excitement in excessive drinking to justify a movement toward self? I simply cannot. Know thyself, and know why you do the things you do.

Now, let's talk about one of the most powerful vibrations out there: gratitude. Be grateful, for it is one of the most substantial emotions available to us. Seriously and sincerely speaking, everything in life is a lesson, especially that which we consider bad experiences. They are avenues in which cracks in our inner world seep out into the universe. They reveal spots in ourselves that need to be given attention so our lives can become lighter and more fulfilling.

Be grateful for beauty, happiness, friends, and family. Don't just be thankful for obvious things like the job promotion that will get you more money. We need to find gratitude in the details. For example, perhaps you catch someone mid-smile as they read a text and think, *What could have possibly stirred such a genuine smile? Something from a lover? A father? A mother or daughter? Maybe their crush asked them on a date? Maybe they got Memorial Day weekend off to go to a music festival with their friends? Maybe their hubby is bringing them a sandwich on the way home from work?*

When I see something like this, I lose my mind in happiness. I'm brought to tears of joy because this is the kind of beauty we must seek out, and in turn, that same beauty will be evoked in us. It's a carefully crafted positive feedback system used to alleviate even the heaviest of souls.

The trick is to stay in the present. On a beautiful, sunny day with a cool coastal breeze blowing from the northwest a few years ago, Santa Barbara delivered as always. People were laughing, smiling, couples held hands, and the majestic courthouse clock tower broadcasted the beauty of our little niche to ships entering the harbor tens of miles away.

I didn't know what had happened, but that day I saw an old lady being wheeled into an ambulance as I drove by. Her body was frail, her skin wrinkled. She was about to die, and she knew it. Her neighbors stood somber and knowingly at the curbside, and you could tell by the serene gait of the paramedics that they knew what was about to happen. But there was also something else. The lady had a peculiar look of acceptance and surrender. There was a peacefulness, a comfort and a slight smirk on her face that said, "Veni, vidi, vici," "I came; I saw; I conquered."

I cried.

Tears slipped from the creases in my eyes, but not from sadness or pity. I cried because I was happy. Weird, right? There was something about the way she carried herself. How could someone about to die seem so content, so at ease? Within a split second, I saw this woman's life flash before my eyes. Adventures in an old world, wild horses galloping across an open plane, scaled mountains into clouded forests. I saw her laughing with friends, having drinks at bars, and swing dancing in beautiful, flowy gowns until the sun came up.

How did I know all this? I didn't. But you don't die that well and have a life of anything less than extraordinary. I cried because I saw hope. I cried because I knew that with this woman's death, everything was right in the world. I quietly thanked her for the elegance and feminine grace she represented. I thanked her for the courage she showed in stepping into her next great adventure with a smile, making room for the next beautiful soul to come to life.

I thanked her because it gave me the perfect example of how to die, and therefore, the perfect example of how to live.

There is beauty to be found in everything and an infinite variety of things to be thankful for when we open ourselves to the infinite possibilities.

When we are not grateful for our lives, we are telling the universe that what we have is not enough. We are broadcasting frequencies into our surrounding space that read "lack and scarcity." In turn, the universe has no choice but to present us with lack and scarcity, not because that's how the world is but because it's what we choose to see. The more powerful the emotion, the more feedback we get from our surroundings. These energies draw certain people in and will direct conversations. They direct consciousness and guide us through synchronistic events. It's not just about saying, "Thank you." It's about mindfully saying, "Yes, this is what I want. Give me more of this." Food grows where water flows.

Now that we are all feeling nice and light, I must hit you with some heaviness. When it comes to using our emotional state of being to broadcast frequencies out into world, our biggest ally isn't actually our conscious thought processes. It's our subconscious. Our conscious mind/ego is lazy. Too much of the same thing and it automatically forces information to the subconscious.

Microsoft Corporation released a study that showed our average attention span is around eight seconds. The conscious mind is spread very thin, especially today. Concentration is harder than ever. The conscious mind is constantly seeking novelty, and it is our subconscious mind that utilizes intuition for those quick-fire decisions that can make or break us.

Not only does our conscious mind get bored easily, but it is also finite. On average, it can only process one thing at a time. If you're a musician, you might be able to get away with upwards of four things at a time, like playing the drums.

What this means is that all the things you can do without thinking about doing are coming from the subconscious mind. Breathing, temperature regulation, the release of certain hormones, and in this case, our intuition all meet this criteria. I've studied human psychology for as long as I can remember, and one of the biggest topics right now is how to influence people's behaviors into buying what they don't actually need. We call this marketing.

Our intuition is tied into our subconscious minds, and psychology shows that the subconscious mind is not necessarily a hard thing to program. Intuition being tied to our subconscious means that our intuition can also be programmed.

Your subconscious mind, rooted to your higher self, has one foot in this three-dimensional reality. It acts here and now with you in this space. It also has a foot on the other side. For example, consider dreams. Your subconscious mind leaves the world in front of your eyes and goes inward. It is doing its best to streamline information from the other side of the veil so you may function at a higher level on this side. However, since it is also attached to this side, in our reality, it is also susceptible to physical reality's trickery.

Your subconscious mind acts like the ocean. Energy put into the ocean is stored by the ocean and radiated back out into the atmosphere. Let's think in terms of heat energy. Ocean science shows that it takes a great deal of energy to heat up the ocean and also to cool it off. This is why coastal climates are much more moderate than inland climates. The ocean acts as a mediator. It never gets overly hot, nor does it get overly cold.

By studying the science of heat energy, we know heat can be transferred from one object to another as long as it is within a certain proximity. Anything near the ocean will, on account of proximity, share in the joy of this relatively moderated climate. Your subconscious mind, being similar to water, acts the same way. In order to program the subconscious mind with our desires, we must be overly diligent with our programming. It must be constant, all day every day, if we wish to instigate a lasting change.

Your subconscious mind mediates everything within proximity of it, just like the ocean does. Think of it as a fail-safe for our internal workings. If our subconscious mind were as fickle as our conscious mind, we would be a mess. We would have no ability to gain momentum or build rhythms in our lives to get anything done or maintain any type of focus.

This is why it is nearly impossible to change another person from their very core. To change what makes a person who he or she is at his or her deepest level is like trying to change the temperature of the deepest part of the ocean by warming the air at the surface. It's just not realistic.

While we can rarely change others or influence them from their core, we can influence their more superficial reactions to the world, the decisions that are a little closer to the surface of the ocean. Our intuition is tied in very closely with our subconscious mind. Those quick-firing decisions of whether we say yes or whether we buy that jacket can easily be defined as our intuition. However, just because we can say we listened to our intuition in making a decision does not mean it is within our best interest, which is what most people assume.

Trust me, if you live in today's world, chances are your intuition has been hijacked.

There are far too many movies, far too many TV shows, magazines and newscasts, billboards and movie advertisements. The trade off-of your subconscious mind is that while it is relentless in its steadfastness, it doesn't distinguish between what is real and what is not. In the same way, your brain's limbic system cannot distinguish between the happiness of you or the happiness you are witnessing from another person; the same parts of the brain light up no matter what.

What this means is that it doesn't matter whether you believe something is true or not. If you are exposed to it long enough, your conscious mind/ego becomes used to it, and out of boredom, the information is kicked down to your subconscious/intuition to be stored and reverberated back out into the world—just like the ocean.

This is not necessarily a psychology book, so I will not dive too deep into various forms of psychological manipulation, but there is one that I find quite interesting. These are some ways in which your mind can be hijacked so you may make more informed decisions in the future.

The first is called *priming*. Priming was studied first by Roger W. Schvaneveldt—an American experimental psychologist with a focus on basic and applied research in cognitive psychology—in the early 1970s. Priming is like planting a seed in someone and being able to remotely cue its growth. You prime people by exposing them to a certain stimulus, a seemingly harmless stimulus that "primes" the individual for a certain reaction to a later stimulus. It's labeled as an "implicit memory effect," which means it slips in past the conscious mind and into the subconscious.

For example, a certain kind of priming called conceptual priming is where language semantics influence decision making. It works like this: I have you sit down at a table to look at a list of words, and

I ask you to tell me the first three words you notice. You pick the word *banana* first, thinking it was your intuition. However, what you didn't know was that I purposely gave you a yellow pen to write with, had yellow inspirational posters next to your desk, and also offered you an apple as you entered the room.

Yellow everywhere, and who doesn't know about apples and bananas? I sure do, and I bet you do, too. This is a test done by psychologists to see how people's decisions can be influenced by manipulating their environment, while still having people believe that the decisions they made were their own.

A similar test was done on wine purchases within a grocery store. The grocery store played either French or German music on alternating days. The idea was to see if the music influenced the type of wine purchased. Do you think there was a correlation? Absolutely. More French wine was purchased when the French music was played and vice versa. Imagine seeing the excitement on a man's face as he comes home to his lover exclaiming, "I just went with my gut on this one. Tonight we're drinking German wine." Was it really his "gut" instinct, though? Or was there a certain unknown factor influencing his actions?

This is why we can't just read one self-help book and "see the light," or see one movie and be inspired to move a mountain. In fact, most of you reading this book will be moved only a few days afterward, if that. Our subconscious minds need much more than a few handwritten notes for substantial changes. The subconscious mind, like the ocean, needs a substantial amount of energy to be manipulated, and that amount of energy only exponentiates the deeper we want the change to happen.

Now, imagine you have been primed every single day since birth to believe certain things and act certain ways. Day in and day out, you are being led to believe that who you think you are is not you at all but a "you" that someone else designed to benefit his or her life and not your own. Imagine that the car you wish to buy, the school you wish to attend, and *your definition of happiness* have all been planted by someone else.

The notions we have can vary so significantly from person to person depending on their own subjective existence and desires. Exposing ourselves to mountains of media propagated from those with their own agendas can lump everything into one category, however, and does not leave room for the infinite options of variation. It causes everyone to have the same exact definition of happiness and the same exact definition for success. Yet, we know that every soul on this planet is unique, and therefore each of our interpretations for these things must vary to some degree.

There is no "one size fits all" to people's purpose and passions, but constantly we hear that money and materialism lead to happiness. Again, when your mind is bombarded with the same thing over and over again, it dumps it off to the subconscious mind, where it is more or less interpreted as reality. Joseph Goebbels, leader of Nazi Germany propaganda, once said, "if you tell a lie big enough and keep repeating it, people will eventually come to believe it." Priming and repetition are two huge factors in the ease for which your intuition is hijacked. Shut off the television, and close the magazines. We have no use for the filtered and monitored garbage that is the majority of daytime TV. It only serves to seduce you in the least enticing of ways. There is hope, however.

You are that hope.

This is where you, the world shaker and paradigm-breaker, come in. You are the kind that creates culture, that vomits truth when lies are crammed down. People like you and me, we say to hell with the lifeless archetypes of previous generations, and we create for something far more magical, for something far more real and true to ourselves and the new direction of the world.

We do it in the way we make our movies and our songs, in the way we dance and the way we make love. Everything we do, we should do because it slapped us across the face at two o'clock in the morning in the middle of the night during a cold sweat, a mountain-sized epiphany that could only have come from the very pit of our own existence, as pure and untainted as midnight dew.

This is true creation, unique to the individual and no one else. We must be diligent on what goes into our minds. Everything we put in front of our faces, symbols, ideas, sounds, words, people, they are all absorbed by the mind and stored within the ocean of our subconscious and then broadcasted back out into the universe.

Constantly be asking yourself if what you are doing is truly in your best interest. Are you angry? Why? What triggered it? Is it real? Is it necessary? You want to buy a certain kind of home? Why? Is the idea yours? Is this home the happiness you know to be true in your heart, or is it only true in last month's popular home magazine? You want to move to California? What is driving you? Whose idea was it, and what does it even matter to you?

This is our opportunity to create the type of life that syncs most closely with who we are, but we have to stay in control of the energies we are broadcasting out into the world, and therefore we must stay in control of those we allow into ours.

Vibration just *is*. It doesn't matter if it is real or imagined. Existence just receives the vibration and answers it with things that match it.

The Debate over "Good" and "Bad"

Have you ever seen a poorly shaped cloud or a wave that didn't crash the "right" way? No, of course not. Clouds cloud, and waves wave. It's what they do. We attract in our lives not by what we think is "good" or by what we think is "bad"; we attract in our lives what our subconscious/conscious minds project into the universe.

These thoughts are not good or bad. They are like waves and clouds. They just are; *we attract by what we are.* And what we are, more or less, is tied to our perceptions of the world. This is why it is so important to understand the law of vibration, to understand that everything in this world emits a frequency, and that in order to get what we want, *we must tie ourselves into that frequency as closely as we can.*

This is why we must give up fighting. The universe wants us to succeed. It wants us to create beauty and life. It wants us to love; love is beauty, and nature adores beauty. I swear on everything that is holy that if you just pursue beauty and genuine passion that everything will be right.

Fighting is obsolete. It's full of fear. It says, "My way of life is threatened" and therefore somehow not right. It says there is not enough in this world for everyone, and lo and behold, what does the world in turn show us? Surprise, surprise—it shows lack. It shows that there is not enough in this world for everyone. It shows all those things we fear most.

One day we will look back and see just how infant-like our society is today. We put so much energy, so much focus and attention into things we do not like and wonder why they continually show. We are constantly creating, whether it be conscious or not. To stop focusing on fighting is to start focusing on building. I can stand on the sidelines and chirp about how much I hate the way the world is or I can start doing things that I love, because that's what the world needs—more people doing what they love, not more people complaining about how poorly misshapen their clouds are.

The world will fix itself when everyone fixes themselves, when everyone lives from a place of abundance, when people start focusing on creating affluence rather than disdaining the circumstances of "their" world.

The world is not a bad place, nor is it a good one. It's neither. The world, like everything else in it, just *is*. And it is not until the introduction of human consciousness that a definition is created, and that definition is damn near magic as it has the possibility of creating a reality that molds to it.

Rain on a wedding day can make one person miserable and another exuberant. People try so hard to polarize good and evil, making a fine line placing this here and that there, and it is a sincere quest for truth. However, extending from source, we are all. We are everything. Therefore, to judge anything as good or evil simply creates limitations. Learning to accept everything for what it is helps expand the human consciousness and limits unnecessary suffering.

Do Not Give in to Astonishment

"Do not give in to astonishment" is a quote from the late Terence Mckenna while on a DMT trip to another universe. He said beings told him not to give in to astonishment while showing him worlds that our most creative minds couldn't possibly come up with. Terence didn't say it straight out, but this idea of not giving in, I believe, is a mechanism in which we can operate beyond the veil of everyday realities.

I want to share a part of my life with you—baseball. I played for most of my childhood and also on a scholarship in college. You see, in baseball, there are certain unwritten rules, things that one must live by, a code among pirates if you will, like not stepping on the fair/foul chalk line markers and not mention *anything* about the pitcher throwing a perfect game even when every soul in the stadium knows exactly what is happening.

And then there are home runs.

When a player hits a home run, he doesn't lose his mind. He doesn't scream and shout and jump up and down in celebration. *A good ball player will act like he's done this before.* He casually strolls the bases, high fives the first base coach, and rounds second base while he brushes dirt from his jersey. He rounds third base with a nonchalant nod to his coach, crosses home plate, and wishes the next batter good luck. He'll say something like, "His fastball moves a bit, but it's pretty hittable," as if he didn't just plant a ball 385 feet down the left field line for the second time this game. Ah, baseball. Such a beautiful, ironic sport.

What does this have to say about the universal law of vibration? Everything. Remember, we attract what our base vibration radiates, which is programmed by both our conscious efforts and our environment. If your view on the world says abundance, the world constantly shows you opportunities for abundance.

There is nothing inherently wrong with being astonished. Astonishment says that we are capable of letting ourselves be overwhelmed with the world. To be astonished is to be dumbstruck, and to be dumbstruck is to surrender to awe. Surrender is a powerful thing. The act of surrender is simply the act of acceptance. It is not the act of giving up anything except for giving up that which is not you. It allows the universe to show you a piece of truth and what's worth living for.

But astonishment is also surprise, and we are anything but surprised at the miracles we get.

Now, back to the home run. What is a player saying by not giving in to astonishment? He is saying that *this always happens whether it's true or not.* He is saying, "I hit home runs. This is what I do. I'm a great athlete, and I do this so often that I don't even get excited anymore. I'm probably gonna hit another home run my next at bat. That's how good I am." He is *programming his subconscious mind.*

Is it true? Is he that good? The beautiful thing about this law is that it does not matter whether it is true or not. All that matters is that he believes it to be true and then repeats so much to the point where he is capable of programming other players around him to believe as well, possibly even more than he does. This sense of confidence is a must, not only for optimal performance in sports but for optimal performance for any mission in life.

If we can't convince ourselves that we are great and that we are more than capable, we lose before we begin. Want to know what we would think when we saw someone hit a homerun and parade around the bases like a twelve-year-old child? We'd think he was a chump. Why? Because he acts like he's never hit a home run before, because he probably hasn't. "Settle down and act like you've done this before," we'd tell him. And it wasn't because we were judgy or mean. It's because great athletes understand something that others don't.

You see, there is a hint of disbelief in astonishment, a hint of "this couldn't possibly be happening." After all, if it was absolutely normal to land humans on Mars, there would be nothing to be excited about. The universe is mind, and if within our minds we believe something shouldn't be possible, then in turn, it won't be possible. This is exponentiated when we cross over into more subtle realities than our own endlessly dense third dimension, for it is in these more ethereal dimensions that mind has a much greater capacity for influence.

Think of dream worlds. Think of how the mind operates within dreams. Have you ever noticed how becoming overly excited in a dream makes you unable to fly or otherwise perform? It happens to me all the time. There I am, Keyth, a happy human, flying through the sky or about to make love to a beautiful faery woman, and *boom*, I realize I'm dreaming. I get excited, and *I give in to astonishment*. The physical laws and regularities of waking life crash into the subtleties of the dream world, and I begin to lose control. It's a battle of the mind. Sometimes I slip and fall back to earth because of the excitement, and sometimes I fly. It all depends on how strong my mind is at the time.

It's a tightrope walk, a benign balance of accepting something as a dream so it can be malleable enough to manipulate with real life practicality. As above, so below, right? Maybe this is how we must operate in the real world. Never believe that anything is so *real* as to not allow it to be anything other than it already is. After all, quantum physics has already found that at the basis of matter exist particles that are both solid and wavelike at the same time. What we see is constant change. As soon as something hits its peak, it begins its downward sprint to death and rebirth.

Maybe *allowing* magic into our lives is the only way magic can exist? Maybe we've had it wrong all along. Maybe seeing isn't believing; maybe believing is seeing.

I don't know, but it keeps me up at night.

How to Be Beautiful

Even though you already are!

I want you to shine an incandescence onto this world of which the cosmos hasn't felt since the first star was formed. I want your magnitude of beauty to shine so bright it casts a shadow long enough to stretch over the faces of history's greatest treasures. You can, and you will. But first things first.

Now this chapter is all about recognizing that everything in existence broadcasts a certain vibration. They are palpable: thoughts, emotions, feelings; they all have measurable wavelengths that can be picked up by the people and things around us.

That said, one of the main focuses of this book is a profound search for truth. The short-lived but incredibly gifted English Romantic poet John Keats said, "'Beauty is truth, truth beauty - that is all ye know on earth, and all ye need to know." It is one hell of a statement, and a piece of your heart will not allow you to pass it up lightly.

I will not only teach you how to be more beautiful but how to attach to one of the most substantial universal truths—the evocation of beauty.

The only downside is that the idea of beauty has been skewed as of late.

Social media and the likes, whether intentionally or not, have framed the idea of beauty merely as something visually appealing, a beautiful woman, a scantily clad man, a $700,000 Ferrari 250 GTO Berlinetta. And it's not that these things don't have an inherent objective beauty to them, only that it does not for the masses portray the limitlessness of beauty. In fact, it does the exact opposite. It shows that beauty is an incredibly rare thing to come by, and while that is definitely a criterion for something beautiful, it is by no means limited to that.

Let's dive a bit deeper.

In order for you to be more beautiful, I must first evoke in you a sense of awe, wonder, and enchantment—not in the obviously beautiful things of the world but in the mundane, for this is the secret to beauty.

All of us wish to appear more attractive. We want to be seen as alive and radiant. We want people to look at us the way we look at our most-prized possessions. And we can. We can do it with ease.

You and I, as sentient beings in this universe, by default, evoke. With our eyes and with our ears, we draw out the vibrations of the cosmos. We draw out the beauty. It's a relationship between the two things, and that relationship is based off of acknowledgment. It is the greatest secret to being the most beautiful person in any room: *acknowledgment*. Surrender to her and she will surrender to you.

In order for us to be beautiful, we must constantly surrender to it. When we make the *choice* to see beauty in this world, we bring out the beauty in ourselves. *We resonate.* There is a part of our brains called the limbic system, and it cannot differentiate between self and others. It means that if you were to tell someone that their eyes are the most radiant shade of green you have ever come across, your brain would not acknowledge that statement as going to someone else. It would think it's happening to itself.

Remember those palpable frequencies we talked about? Your acknowledgment in the exterior world will evoke the internal, and a frequency will then be broadcasted from you like a beacon.

You must be able to find yourself mesmerized by the beauties of the world.

My friends, this is where we turn into beauty-seekers. It's the only thing that will save you. This type of emotional energy is incredible. It draws us in because it is beautiful. It is home. By default, you become beautiful—not in the "pretty face," "nice eyes" way, but in the way you make people feel when they are in your presence.

You become a magnet for the beautiful experiences in your life because you have made a choice to bear witness to all forms of beauty. It's almost a way of the universe saying, "Thank you for the acknowledgment. Here, have some more!" This concept is nothing new to us. When studying romantic relationships, we find that in showing appreciation to someone for something they did, even a simple and sincere thank you can in turn inspire that person to continue with it.

It's like when your beautiful lover comes home and smothers your face with soft kisses of gratitude for making him or her a meal—it makes you happy. It makes you happy that you can do something *so little* for someone, yet it brings them a profound sense of happiness. Can you imagine all the other kinds of thank yous to dish out for a lover and how that might influence the romance of your relationship? Positive feedback loops galore!

The point I'm getting at is that giving is receiving, as it always is and always has been. Give it away and it will all come back. The world is perfect in that way. *When you choose to see beauty in everything,* to acknowledge and give it a witness, the world will say thank you.

Tell your lover you think he or she is as radiant as the sun, and watch him or her shine even brighter for you. Tell the stranger on the street that his or her shoes look extra fly and watch him or her strut a bit sharper. Tell a child his or her painting is a beauty unlike this world has ever seen and watch him or her turn into Van Gogh.

It is also important not to put a cap on how much you see. Let your conjuring awareness bring forth an oasis in the dry desert of today's overly demanding world. There is no quota for how much you can witness, no boundary to wonder. It is the only way our world will be saved. Let beauty fall as much on the setting sun as with the falling of a leaf, with the laughter of a child, two strangers hugging, or young romance. It all has its place, and it all needs a witness, our awareness acting as water for its growth.

You have the power to create simply by *choice.* It doesn't take any more than that. That is what the yogis mean. It's what the new age folk are trying to preach. That there is an abundance of anything in this world, and we evoke that abundance as if it were an art. Because it is.

Alas! I digress. This section was supposed to be all about you.

Why is it that by being a treasure hunter of beauty, you become more beautiful? Because the more you find yourself seeking out beauty and acquiescing the artistry of the mundane, the more your own unique allure is teased from your soul. And my god, does it show in the purest of ways! It becomes in you almost a naive spontaneity. You become a slave to your emotions in the best of ways. You begin to lose yourself to the moment, having conversations that you never would have thought to have and finding yourself in the most peculiar yet invigorating circumstances.

You begin to do things you never thought you would be doing. Headed to the grocery store, you say? How about you just keep driving to the beach and watch the sunset? After all, how long has it been since you last sat and let the rays of a sleeping sun warm your face? You were about to smash that poor spider in the corner, were you? How about you admire the symmetry of those wild, ever-present eyeballs?

I promise, practice this one thing, and you will be able to find beauty in a doornail, for everything represents something grander. Everything has a past, a present, and a future. It was, is, or can be a part of something bigger. Almost *anything* can be found to be beautiful. Even sadness is something that should bring a certain type of joy to you.

Sadness beautiful?

If I don't make you a believer after the next few paragraphs, I have failed you. Sadness is a necessary component of life. It simply must exist. Happiness exists, and therefore so must its opposite. Imagine what happiness would be like without sadness. Nothing to define, nothing to compare to—sameness forever. It would be an awfully dull experience if that were the case, but it is not. Sadness is here, and it is one of the most powerful teachers of beauty that one can receive.

Sadness is a reminder, albeit a selfish one. It is a reminder of how happy experiences in life have made us. This is why happiness and sadness are two sides of the same coin. They both offer us insights on the same thing on our never-ending, unique subjective experiences. In other words, sadness is telling you that at one point, you were *just as happy as you are sad right now.* This is a rhythmic compensation that is built into the structure of life. It's like being on a swing. The higher you swing forward, the higher you swing back.

But there is hope! I will teach you how to overcome sadness—to eradicate it from your life, forever. Are you ready?

The way to overcome all sadness in your life is ... You don't.

To get rid of sadness would be to get rid of happiness, for again, they are one and the same thing. What we can get rid of, however, are the paradigms we hold against sadness, and in turn we will find a beauty like no other.

Here's how to turn sadness into beauty.

First, stop labeling sadness as "bad." Sadness is neutral in its existence on this plane. It isn't until you interact with the emotion via your thoughts that any desirable or undesirable outcome is evoked. Strip away any and all preconceived notions on sadness, so you may lay down a healthier perspective more relative to your new direction.

Now that your "sadness" is without name and definition, I'm going to share with you some sad memories from my own life. I want you to see these different circumstances and—this is crucial— before you have any reactions to these circumstances, I want you to remind yourself what the goal is here, which is to seek beauty. Let's begin.

As I hear a song that reminds me of my old sweetheart, I imagine her screaming my nickname, then sprint from the doorstep of her house half a block away, jump, and cling on to me like the most adorable spider monkey in the western hemisphere. What's the sadness? She broke up with me, and I'm still not even sure why.

A second memory is from when my grandfather, who was like a father to me, passed away. From him I got a lot of my favorite characteristics as a person. He helped me grow a pumpkin that won first prize at a fair when I was twelve. He taught me how to drive a stick shift at age ten (although I suspect that was more because he didn't want to drive the way home from school), and he called me his "baby baby" at the age of twenty-three, something I didn't mind one bit. He died while i was away at college and I had no chance to say good-bye.

Below, I will analyze my thoughts on what happened in my mind while I wrote that last section. Pay close attention to the following paragraph.

Halfway through writing that little segment, I started to realize that the only things that were actually making me sad were in reality happy thoughts. The excitement in my girl's eyes and voice after not seeing me for weeks and the joy my grandfather felt from spending time with me, helping me learn and grow.

Sadness is, first and foremost, a reminder. It reminds you of little snippets of your life that felt *perfect*, that make you feel like your life would be perfect if it just stayed like that forever. Sadness is funny that way. It somehow manages to vividly draw on our most treasured memories and drown our hearts in nostalgic fervors of woe. And during these emotions, I found myself becoming softer, more empathetic, and more compassionate. Have you ever felt like those who experience the most pain are some of the most empathetic to our hurts? There is a reason for that.

I started to see that my happiness came from feeling a connectedness to other people. I found that my experiences made me more empathetic to those in my life who might have gone through similar things. What surprised me most while thinking of these memories was that my lips were pulled back in the softest and sincerest of smiles. A part of me was acknowledging these moments and thanking them for having happened in the first place.

These thoughts reminded me that it was only because these events and people had made such a positive, loving impact on my life that I could experience such sadness. But it was not a reminder solely of past events but of future as well.

And we've come full circle. My acknowledgment of the beautiful parts of the sadness made the experience beautiful in its own melancholic way. So this will be your job. Take the sadness that you have tried to hide away, and find out what it is reminding you of. Find out where the happiness is hiding.

It is easy to become overwhelmed with sadness that has not yet been processed or fully acknowledged, however, so it is important to let it run its course. Cry, scream, and let the energy flow through you. Keeping it in can wreak physical havoc on your body. We don't want that. It can lead to depressed states. What you do now is say thank you. Yes. *You say thank you.* Thank you for the happiness you once brought me. Thank you for allowing me the opportunity to *feel* something as powerful as I did. Thank you for showing me a piece of beauty that some search their whole lives for. Thank you for showing me the caliber of happiness that I am capable of and for allowing me a chance to dream about an even bigger and better future. To show sadness is vulnerability, and I cannot stress the importance of that. To be vulnerable allows the ones around you to in turn invoke their own sense of empathy. It allows people to connect with you and see something real, which a lot of people rarely get to experience, especially in today's perfectionist society.

The point is, happiness turns to sadness and then *back* to happiness. All things at some point must return to their origin—up and down, back and forth, a coming and going of vibrations. Nothing lasts forever, and that is what makes it so beautiful. That's what makes you so beautiful.

CHAPTER 5

The Law of Polarity

We forget that things can only be things when there is
something which is not a thing, the space.

—*Chris Matakas*

GREEN SHINY FROGS BOUNCE up and down on top of soft, slick lily pads. Their emerald sheen flickers in the moonlight. Their incandescent croaks bounce off the hard branches and paper-like leaves within their murky niche. Each sound gives definition to the dark world around them.

Are the lily pads really that soft, though? They're hard enough to use as a spring but soft enough to evoke softness from our own fingertips. And since we're on the subject, is the lily pad really that slick? I mean, the frogs seem to handle it just fine. To their feet, the lily pads must have a sturdy grip.

How about that murky, dark niche of theirs? I'm sure they can see just fine. How rude of me to call their refulgent, shining oasis murky. Excuse us humans, poor little green friends, for we know not what we speak.

Poor? Little?

How easy it is to forget. After all, to the smaller insects, you are mighty and ferocious hunters snapping your whip-like tongues hundreds of feet long and snatching the souls of helpless prey as they soar through the sky.

The law of polarity is a fun game, isn't it? I was being as facetious as I could, but in all realness, there was nothing wrong with either side of the conundrums. The lily pads were both soft and hard depending upon what it was that was trying to evoke it. The swamp was both murky and luminous depending upon whose eyes were watching. The frogs, while tiny to us, must look to a fly like blue whales with two hundred feet long tongues that devour bodies in the blink of an eye.

The universe is nothing until the invocation by consciousness, and really, it's true. The universe is darkness until its light is thrust upon the eye and the world is lit up via the mind. Without one, we cannot have the other. This is the byproduct of the law of polarity.

We as humans evoke. And in that evocation of existence, two polar opposites for each "thing" that reveals itself manifests. Everything that is created within the mind of The All must manifest itself on all planes, both a positive and a negative side. There must be an experience of something, anything, and without the opposite of one thing, there would be no experience. There would just be sameness.

Within the infiniteness of the space between these poles is where we find ourselves. Our lives are riddled with subjectivity, and the capacity for discovery is shy on everlasting.

Think of a thermometer. There is nowhere on the thermometer that says this is hot and this is cold. It is only a gauge with which we can determine the *degree* of heat energy present within a location.

Now, imagine that little red line as it swings from one side to the other. You will notice that the red line never actually changes in character. It is always the same thing, only varying in *degree*. What I mean to say is that the red line will always be the red line.

Hot and cold are the exact same thing. They are two different ways of seeing energy.

This applies to *everything*. Opposites are exactly the same. All that changes is the degree of the thing in mention. When that "thing" slides more prominently to one side, we give it a name, and when it swings back in the other direction, we call it something else. And when it hangs somewhere in the middle long enough, we go to war over it.

Depressing, I know.

But it is still the same thing. After all, all is one, right? Everything emanates from source.

It's the same way we manifest anything in our lives. Everything comes from source, so it all must be the same, in a sense. What happens is the degree to which something begins to manifest varies almost infinitely.

If a degree of happiness can stretch to incomprehensible heights, what does that say about the degree of happiness in the other direction? Does it make it sadness? It might, but one person's sorrow is another's blessing, so that can't always be the case. The problem is, most don't realize that opposites are the same and therefore fail to realize that transmuting emotions is exceedingly more manageable than we previously realized.

There really is no cold, only an absence of heat, no darkness, just an absence of light, and no sadness but an absence of happiness. We begin to distinguish emotions and thoughts. We begin to observe that whenever we see something as "not good," it's not that it's "bad," but that there's a lack of something "good." This awareness, this new paradigm of thought, *will make all the difference in the world*.

Now we have fun.

Polarity allows us to relish in *difference*. Polarity is the reason a red rose is so beautiful in a field of white. It's why a white flower is so beautiful in a field of red. Polarity allows a stark contrast for a truly individualistic involvement with the world and everything in it.

If there was not an opposite for us to compare to, how would we truly be able to embody an experience and appreciate it for what it really is? How would we know pleasure without pain, happiness without sorrow? How would we know anything if everything was the same? What experience would we leave this world with if there was nothing but one thing to experience?

Woe is me!

If I gave you a green apple to eat and it was from the same tree for the entirety of your life and at the end asked you if green apples are good, you might ask, "Good as compared to what?"

And rightly so, for you have only ever eaten green apples. How should you know if they are really good? They might be disgusting compared to red apples, but you have never experienced red apples, so you cannot have an opinion. You might think green apples are good solely because you've had them for your entire life, which seems an awfully boring and dull way to come to appreciate something. They are just apples and you eat them; onto the next life.

The point of life is to be passionate—to live, dream, and play, and to do it all within the intricacies of personified emotion and energy. We learned from our frog friends that there is no such thing as "good" and no such thing as "bad," "big," or "small." All these concepts represent the same thing—the difference residing in *the degree in which it manifests.*

Everything has an opposite—*everything,* including our minds and mental states. This is how we apply the law of polarity for mental transmutation to change our internal mechanics and therefore our universe.

If the universe is mental, and creation begins with the mind, it is the mastery of mind that will allow us mastery of the universe and mastery of creation. Our mental states and emotions—which are incredibly powerful tools for manifestation—can be changed and manipulated, *transmuted from one degree to another.* This is the real sorcerer's stone—not physical lead into gold, but mental lead into gold.

Perspective, perspective, perspective.

Perspective is what we must focus on. Part of Einstein's theory of relativity is that everything is in relation to everything else. Everything is and isn't at the same time.

There are two sides to every coin.

We know this to be true but not necessarily how to apply it. Yet, in learning how to apply it, we rise above the swinging pendulum of lower vibrational states. We have learned in previous chapters that it is our perception of circumstances that defines the absolute outcome of a happening. This means that we are able to, more or less, dictate the outcome of an event based solely on how we choose to interpret that event within our minds. If we can find something useful, then the event is not a total loss, and we learn from it.

You learn how to manipulate your mind so it works *for* you, not against you. That's why you are here. Let's practice with the mental state of courage and fear. If we accept the paradigm in which these states are actually the same, only varying in degree, we can see that neither one is good or bad because in actuality, they are the same.

Most people avoid fear. They avoid what frightens them and seamlessly scant themselves out of situations that could transform their lives. If only they made the leap, if only they could trust the blind jump into nothingness and let their wings unfold on the way down. But alas, most of them stay on the shores of safety, never to allow their boats to cast into the uncertainty of the ocean.

But not you.

You understand that fear and courage are the same thing and are driven by a new kind of paradigm—one that says to follow excitement recklessly into the world. This is the new reaction we aim for: when you find yourself in a truly fearful situation—and you will—understand that the fear is only presenting you with an opportunity to be great. Instead of resisting fear, all you have to do is promote the movement up the scale to courage. Begin to notice that fear was never really fear; *it was only a manifestation of a lack of courage.*

Brimming with this newfound potential, we can laugh at how much of worry is false flagged and misconstrued. We can turn into thieves of life, like Robin Hood and his comrades: poor in materials but rich in spirit, merriment, laughter, and drinks all around. What is there possibly to be afraid of? Failure? Death, perhaps? Death is a man we shake hands with every time we step out the door. Look at him and say, "Hi there, Death, what adventures shall we embark upon today!" How can we possibly be afraid to die when we have lived such rich lives? Like Peter Pan once said, to die would be an awfully great adventure, and who knows, you might even end up back home.

It may seem straight-forward and almost too easy. "After all," you might say, "if it were just a matter of sliding it up the scale, then why can I not just think *courage* and automatically be courageous. Isn't mind all?"

Great question.

This is about having an experience. Get the idea out of your head that all you have to do is think something into existence. The secret is that that is *not* the secret. Thinking is far less than half the battle. We need not take the quick route all the time. Life isn't about a destination, it's about an experience, and that experience is found in the journey. Thus, sit down, be quiet, and enjoy the ride.

To understand that fear and courage are of the same making means that in every situation in which you are fearful, *you are given an opportunity to be brave.* How can it not be? Courage and fear are same, are they not? So why wouldn't every situation in which you are terrified present you with an opportunity to be brave?

You only ever have the opportunity to be brave when you are afraid.

Ah! One of the more beautiful paradoxes in this enigmatic universe. Are you beginning to see the beauty and necessity of the law of polarity? *One side cannot exist without the other.* The two are tied in a symbiotic dance across the perpetual horizon of creation. This is why you cannot simply think something and have it happen.

Thinking is mostly harmful anyway, but what about feeling? Now that's something we can use. You don't become courageous by simply thinking it; you must actually do. *You must involve yourself in the process.*

Your chance to shine is given to you daily, *but it is only a chance,* contingent on the choices that follow, contingent on whether you are brave enough to take the leap. Opportunities for courage are constantly provided, but they are only opportunities, not guarantees.

So jump.

And do not think something is wrong if no matter how hard you try, you just can't seem to get rid of the terror in your mind that plants your feet to the ground. That feeling will never leave. Your job isn't to control your mind or the fear it creates. Fear will *always* be there to torment you, but that's okay. Keep your eye ever on the spectrum for that which you wish to conjure. Hold courage in your mind's eye constantly.

Realize that focusing your awareness continually on courage in every situation no matter what the cost will lead your essence toward courage. But please, I urge you, understand that *courage is still fear*. To be able to operate from a place of courage means fear must also be present in order to define that which is courage.

To say you have finally reached the substantiality of courage is to say you have reached the end of the line. Thanks to the mechanisms of The All, there is no end of the line. Courage to you one day is a child's task on the next, and so ever onward. The difference in degree between two phenomenon, in this case courage and fear, is nigh on infinite.

There is no beginning and no end to how courageous one can be, which means there is no end or beginning to how *fearful* one can be. This means that we continuously, until the end of days, can climb the ladder of courage into unfathomable dimensions.

If fear is king, failure is its most strategic general. But I will show you how to use fear against itself so that it will never hold you back.

In fact, sensing fear from now on should encourage you to take twice as much action as before. Here it is.

If you are failing, you are successful. Simple. Now let's dive deeper.

Failure and success are the same thing. So in this case we polarize ourselves onto a mental state that is more conducive to creating the types of lives we wish to live.

Let's look at the "positive" side. Do you want to know what it means when you are doing things right all the time? Always having things go your way and never having a moment of hardship in your life? It means you are never trying anything new, and if so, it becomes difficult to evolve and grow as a human.

There is absolutely nothing wrong with failure. It is a necessity of life. It means you're expanding. It means you have found a new place that you can now explore. Can you imagine all the beautiful lessons you learned from life through your failures? You learned who you were, how you act in the face of adversity, how far you've come, and how much further you still have to go. Your failures are just as much a road map of your entire life as are your successes. In fact, I'd argue they are even more.

To avoid failure is to avoid damn near half of life's experiences. When you were a child, you tried to walk, probably hundreds of times before finally getting it right. Soon after, you tried to talk with the same amount of success. But you got through it, right? You always do.

Stumbling on huge decisions in your life because of the fear of failure is one of the most somber things you will ever have to look back upon while lying on your deathbed.

I can assure you, when you first try something new, you will most likely fail. It's brand new. Do you really expect to perform like your idol?

It's far more logical to expect failure, so why not do it? Why not expect it and even embrace it? Don't let it come as a surprise. Smile at it. Welcome it! Say, "Hi there, failure, fancy seeing you again! It seems I have taken to a new course in life, and it seems you are as relentless as ever!"

After a while, it will turn into your friend. You will begin to share drinks and laugh with fear at the local bar, reminiscing about all the times it *almost* got you. Failure can be *anything* you want it to be. It is more or less like the nothingness of the universe from which everything else manifests.

Because of that, we have the power to transform the fear of failure into an ally. It will soon greet you at your door like a friend, obnoxiously and sarcastically shouting, "Congratulations, I see you have been trying something new lately! I hope you crash and burn, you schmuck!"

That's all it is—a friendly reminder of your inevitable and perpetual growth into the limitless future. Fear will take you to places you never thought possible. Hunt it down, for it will not bring you down. It will lift you up.

Straight through failure is success. Don't run from it, and don't cower from it. Greet it. It is the doorway to your most fulfilling enterprises.

Like I said before, as long as courage is around, so too will fear be. Therefore, I challenge you to (metaphorically) stare directly into the sun, no matter how bright it may burn, so that the shadow is always cast behind you. The brighter your sun burns, the darker the shadow will be, and the more terrifying the fear.

But you're up for the challenge. You can do anything and be anything because you are a spec of consciousness with the freedom of nothingness. You now have knowledge that most don't, to polarize yourself exactly where you need to be in order to get to where you want. You are infinite.

It's interesting how this emotion works, this fear. It is completely indifferent, yet we treat it like an ominous entity. We let it dictate our lives. We turn into passive machines perplexed and puzzled, only by chance stumbling onto our hopes and dreams, if ever.

But not anymore. Now we happen to the world instead of the world happening to us. Now we live on purpose.

CHAPTER 6

Law of Rhythm

Life is like dancing. If we have a big floor, many people will dance. Some will get angry when the rhythm changes. But life is changing all the time.

—*Miguel Angel Ruiz*

LIFE SWAYS BACK AND forth, to and fro. It's a ceremonious celestial dance, a universal rhythm that we play along to both consciously and subconsciously. It moves toward us at the speed of light and then dashes away as if to say, "No, not this time!" Everything is musical in nature—a rhythmic dance intertwined within life.

Not one part of the universe escapes rhythm. All energies manifested sway from one pole to the opposite. Nothing escapes this law. Just like a swing, rhythm compensates all actions. No event may happen without an equal reaction, or swing, in the opposite direction. Push something far enough forward and it will swing back with near-equivalent force.

Just like music, *timing* is a crucial element in life. If we agree that there are good times to do certain things, then we also must accept that there are bad times to do certain things. There are times to act and times to reflect; there are times to advance, and there are times to withdraw.

We learn these processes from observing the rhythms of the natural world. The sun rises and it sets; the tide races up the shore in greeting and slips away in farewell. Empires rise and they fall. Our emotions are no different.

Understanding this law allows us to appreciate contrast within our lives. The law of polarity and the law of rhythm work in tandem to give definition to our individual existences. When we witness the swing of life in action, we witness true definition of polar opposites, defining them like a brand new 4k TV.

Only instead of seeing the definition on a screen, we see it in the processes of our external and internal worlds. Opposites are absolutely essential in defining life and our experiences in it. The trick is to not allow ourselves to become transfixed into any particular polarity. It is to expect change and simply bear witness. We do not have to tune into their frequencies.

The law of rhythm operates *within* the law of polarity, constantly bouncing back and forth between the two poles. Everything in life has an ebb and flow, a coming and going, birth, growth, death, rebirth, and so on.

In the previous chapter, we learned that everything has its polar opposite and that polar opposites are actually the same thing, differing only in degree. Rhythm operates between the two extremes of that same thing. Rhythm is a pulse. It keeps things alive and real. It allows all things a chance to return. It manifests on all planes: physical, mental, and emotional, economies, the natural world, and celestial bodies. It's all the same.

You see, life must have movement. It must have rhythm. It is one of the fundamental principles that allows us a way to truly experience the universe. There is no true cessation to any process. Just like with polarity, we only understand mesmerizing joy because we have experienced terrifying sorrow. It is the same way when it comes to colors. The color red, for example, is merely a certain wavelength, a dancing frequency spiraling within a certain framework, a *rhythm* that allows the wave of light to represent a different color solely off its own particular dance.

The law of rhythm is also displayed on a much grander scale, for example, when great empires rise and fall and the way seasons constantly flow in and out of each other. Stars form and blast energy out into the universe, only to ultimately die and collapse inward on themselves, only to bounce back again as the power of a supernova.

Celestial bodies dance around the universe tied together by the magic of gravity. What's important here is not so much *that* everything swings from one side to the other but *why* everything swings from one side to the other. Furthermore, what can we do with that knowledge?

The law of rhythm says everything in the universe acts like a pendulum, and depending upon the swing of one direction, we can easily determine what will be happening on the opposite side. This is one of the major points of this chapter—to be able to recognize that for every action there is an equal and opposite reaction.

Nothing new, right? This is what we will call compensation. It's a counterbalance. The swing of a pendulum in one direction will determine the swing in the opposite.

Influencing the Swing of the Mental State

Now that we know the law of rhythm is like a swing, we know that just like swings, it can be influenced. If we have a pendulum and want it to go a little further, have a little more energy, we simply lift our side up a little higher.

The manipulation on one end allows the other end to reciprocate the action relatively, allowing us to tamper with the extremities of life. This may be good, and it may be bad. It all depends on your perception of the word and how conscious you are of using it.

So, now we apply it to the mind. We say that the capacity to experience a certain emotion is dictated based off how much the mind has expanded in the opposite direction. It's an interesting thought, isn't it, that we are capable of experiencing something only when the opposite exists. In other words, the person who is keen to extreme joy is also keen to extreme suffering. Empaths struggle with this constantly.

In the same way the rhythm of pedaling keeps your bike centered, rhythm provides balance as well. If you stop the pedaling, you fall. This is the necessity of rhythm. It might seem a bit dismal at first, but on some level, we know this to be true.

Think of all the harshness and various obstacles one must overcome in order to become great - I cannot recall a legend or hero who rose to great heights through whimsical feats. With great achievement comes great sacrifice. We all know that.

Rhythm compensates. It is in darkness that light shines the brightest. Likewise, the person who feels little pain is also subject to very little happiness. We see this in relationships and matters of a broken heart. The more in love with someone we are, the more traumatized we are when we lose that person. And imagine a person who has locked himself out and shut emotional doors from potential love to protect himself. Yes, he loses the risk of being hurt and therefore is able to keep his heart intact and happiness within moderation, *but the capacity for love is equally compromised.* It is also held within moderation.

There is always compensation with our actions, and the rule is this: within each individual, the capacity to feel an experience is balanced by its opposite swing.

Today's culture requires that we constantly strive for happiness, and I apologize if I have given off the same impression. If I have, let me correct myself. To always be happy would violate the natural swing of life, the natural rhythm. This is something every person must absolutely understand.

Happiness and sadness exist simultaneously and are of the same making. But instead we have created a society in which we must cover up and hide our emotions. If we are having a bad day, we must shake it off, put on a fake smile, and pretend like everything is okay.

We wouldn't want to attract "bad" things by talking about our sadness, would we?

We are no longer allowed to really feel our emotions. But emotions are here to show us meaning and give us lessons. We only want one side of the spectrum, and as a result, we cut out an entire section of our lives, constantly hidden under the blanket of false optimism. Novelist and philosopher Aldous Huxley's novel *Brave New World,* he writes about something called "soma pills," which refers to how people constantly look for quick fixes to their emotional states. He explains how these people end up becoming shells and lose the capacity to feel altogether.

When I was younger, I would lay on the cold tile floor before getting into the shower, as far away from the shower as I could.

I did this because I knew that the longer I felt the cold and the more I would allow it to settle into my bones, the more invigorating the warmth of the water would be when it finally hit my skin. The cold, dirty floor prior to the cleanliness of the hot shower was a godsend.

There was a rebound effect, like slamming a basketball against a floor. The harder you throw it down, the further up it bounces. This is what happens when we do not hide our sadness, so forget about society and its senseless quest for perfection. We will not reach it, and we will only create unnecessary depression in its quest. Instead, substitute perfection for adaptability and progress. That is all we can ask for.

After all, can you imagine how depressing it is to have to cover up your depression? In today's society, there's something "wrong" with you if you have it, but I would say it is more wrong when you can't express or let it flow through you instead of trapping it inside.

Ironically, when we begin to normalize sadness, we will be happier. We will allow the natural ebb and flow of the emotion to take its place. We'll no longer hide from it but face it. We'll learn from it and therefore take that knowledge and use it as a self-manifested propulsion system to launch the swing of the pendulum back to the spectrum of "happy."

To experience sadness is to fully experience its counterpart. Rhythm compensates. This is the reason why we must not hide our sadness by covering it up and pretending like it doesn't exist. Our sadness has an important role and deserves just as much respect and understanding as happiness. To understand one is to understand the other.

Embrace it, see it, feel it. Sadness, and all emotions in general, are merely natural responses to life. We must expect it. Probe its nature, see where it is coming from, explore what people or situations influence it.

Cutting off sadness is like trying to cross the country in a wagon with no map. Our emotions are indicators of certain frequencies that we find ourselves in and indicators of how we react. In order to navigate this world via its subtler vibrations, we must become more aware of our mental states of being.

That's why activities like meditation and yoga are so beneficial. They force us to take an objective viewpoint of our minds to make an accurate and useful interpretation of our circumstances without judgment.

If we constantly hide from "negative" emotions, however, and pretend that they don't exist, we force a willed ignorance to nearly half the things in our lives. As a result, we stumble forward haphazardly, lucky to have gained any ground or momentum at all. Thus, explore the sadness. Write it out on paper, and then light it on fire. Talk with people you trust. Create a personified image in your head of what you think the sadness is, and then smother it with love.

I promise, this approach to life will change your world. We must walk through the fire so that it can burn off all our rough edges and then birth a phoenix on the other end. It's a purification process.

Part of understanding rhythm is understanding the need to truly feel out an emotion *when* we experience it.

The person who is able to observe his or her emotions while free from attachment conquers this law. This is the way in which we avoid the imminent swing of the pendulum. We cannot stop the swing of life, but we can, with some work, rise above the swing and let it sway underneath us. Meditation, yoga, silent retreats, and mindful thought observation all give us the skills necessary to see the mind for what it really is: something that is *not* us. And because it is *not* us, we don't have to attach ourselves to it when it changes its swing.

The mind may change, but that does not mean we have to change with it. Each of us has experienced the same thing. We go through periods of extreme motivation followed by periods of extreme laziness. We can never seem to maintain a constant framework of the mind that we deem desirable, but that is just something the mind does. Nothing escapes the swing of rhythm.

So we accept it. We surrender to the mind's fickleness, to avoid a kind of doubling up of negative emotions when the mind does something we don't like. Do not try to control the mind. That is nearly impossible. It will come back to you when it comes back to you.

Let's get back to timing and utilize a concept from a different chapter: the law of correspondence.

What do we know about rhythm off hand? Music! Rhythm is music, and music is rhythm. When we hear a tasty song with a steady bass, crisp snaps, and sizzling snares, it moves our souls! There's no way we can stay still when we hear a beautiful tune held steady for our hearts to hear. In music, timing is everything. Without it, it wouldn't make sense. Since we know timing is crucial for music, and rhythm is music, we can use timing to discover the secrets of the law of rhythm and apply them to other areas of our life. Once again we may use this information to become the chess *players* rather than the pieces.

Rhythm means timing, and timing means there are appropriate times for things and there are inappropriate times for things. Apply this to your mental states—a lack of motivation doesn't have to mean lack of motivation. It could mean that it's time to refocus and reorganize your thoughts. Maybe it's not a time to thrust out into the world but to sit back and meditate on the progress you have made and contemplate whether you need to make any adjustments for the next swing of momentum.

We need to understand that you can't *always* be motivated because that would mean you're only ever having *one* experience and not its opposite. We know by nearly all the other laws that that is simply not possible. So if it were me, instead of getting upset for lacking motivation and making my emotional state even worse, I'd say, "Relax. What you are doing is bigger than an emotional state. It's your purpose, your passion, your job. It doesn't rely on something as fickle as the mind and its swings. I do what I do regardless of my circumstance."

The interpretation is up to you because your experience is yours. You are free to produce an outcome that is more in line with your own beliefs and paradigms, as long as you are observing objectively and not letting it dictate your state of being.

The emotions do not define us, only our state of being does. We can imagine that there are two states of focus, or consciousness. Raise your consciousness with your awareness so that the compensation of rhythm does not affect you, akin to rising above the swinging pendulum. It still swings, but you are no longer in its path. You are above with a much clearer vantage point.

The law of rhythm is very simple. It lets us see that everything has its time and place. It says that we cannot have our cake and eat it. If we have one thing, we must lack another. Olympic runners train for endurance and lose speed, or train for speed and lose out on endurance.

We more or less pay a price for what we have and get paid for what we do not. Think of the modern world, advanced in technology and an "easier" way of life. Is it really easier? We have better medicine but have seen a rise in disease and decay. Our lives are longer, but suicide rates are higher than ever before. Have we traded quality for quantity?

We have apartments that touch the ocean and reach the sky. They are such beautifully sculpted homes, but each in its own little box, its own little cubby. We have traded community for privacy, and cut ourselves off from the world in the name of luxury, and we are finally beginning to see the cost.

A poor person will never understand what it's like to have the finest food from around the world at the edge of his finger tip, but the rich will never enjoy the blissful appetite of the beggar. Such is life.

Without rhythm nothing would be real. Rhythm is as close to the substantiality of existence as is anything else. The cadence of life is a blueprint. It is a manifestation of some internal driving force keeping everything in harmony, keeping everything alive.

Think back to music and of its counts, one-two, one-two, one-two. Can you feel the flux? Can you feel the *difference* between the one and the two? It is that difference -- that rythym -- that keeps things in...balance. It's the heart of creation that pumps energy in waves from source.

Now try this. Instead of "one-two," try, "one-one."

Ready?

Go.

One, one, one, one, one—did you feel the rhythm dissolve? The bounce is gone. The *life* is gone. Differences drive forth harmony. It's always a relationship between two different things. It's the space in between, *the nothingness,* that gives space for the complexities of life. So they can define themselves in all their splendid beauty.

There must be space for creation to happen. We must allow for a certain amount of nothingness for something else to fluctuate, and it's in the rhythm of the space where it happens. Rhythm is life, and life is rhythm.

Duality actually *creates the whole*. Duality shows oneness and oneness that inevitably reveals duality. One cannot exist without the other. This is the magic of rhythm, and of the universe. Rhythm is showing us how the flow operates between polar opposites.

This means that well-executed timing and rhythm is a key ingredient to make anything work, and more importantly, make anything *last*. Maintain rhythm and we maintain life. What I've come to learn about these universal laws is that they operate independent of our views on them. Rhythm is neither good nor bad; it simply is.

This means that a well-executed plan following these laws, such as rhythm, will be a success, even if it is terribly detrimental to our well being. But learning how to see these swings, and how to create our own rhythmic movements in life, will help stabilize us so that we have a solid platform for our endeavors. It will help us utilize the most powerful driving forces available to us: momentum.

How to Utilize Rhythm

Dance, play, be jovial, and lighthearted! Look, I get it. Life can be very serious. Even in the presentation of this book, I find myself constantly going too far with the sobriety of the content, constantly going back and rewording sentences as to not come off too pretentious or matter-of-fact.

The truth is that we mustn't take anything in life too seriously, not even this book—not because it isn't serious, but because in order to dance with the sway of life we must be light on our feet. We must constantly be ready to skip around the enigmatic matrices of life so we are not smashed upon the rocks as the tide rises in its rhythmic dance.

"Never serious, always sincere," as British philosopher Alan Watts put it. Play is light. It requires a certain amount of space to exist, a certain freedom of expression. That expression is limited when bogged down with the rigidity of "seriousness."

I previously mentioned the energy or energies we bring into situations. Our energy is palpable, and to broadcast that energy into events is to manipulate those events with the energy.

We must also be able to dance, to relate to the world and its processes as a tango between us and everything else. Remember, understanding rhythm means we can distinguish between periods of ups and downs, *between the swing of the pendulum*. As a result, we can practice timing within our actions and mind-sets.

What else does timing involve? Dance. Is rhythm not the most important part of dancing? Of making music? As I write this, I watch a woman walk down the street with a child resting lazily on her hip. She seems to be lost in thought, aimlessly gazing into each of the shops and pondering god knows what.

Ahead of her, a street musician plays a lively folk song and sings. And still, with the spaced look in her eyes and caught somewhere deep in the depths of her mind, the girl begins to dance. She has a subtle shift in dynamic, like she is being moved by invisible strings, and the closer she gets to the rhythm, the more assertive her dance becomes. She focuses in on the child as to say, "Hey! You hear that!" She stops in front of the musician and begins to dance. Her thoughts and awareness have solidified on the music, and rhythm takes over her body. It's such beautiful sight.

A well-crafted song provides an irresistible movement to erupt from inside. *Put rhythm back into your lives.* You know how powerful it is. You know how moving it is. You know how much of an integral part to our existence it is.

It would be a shame not to utilize this force consciously. Get familiar with your movements. Get familiar with your patterns and rhythms, and use them to your advantage. Ride the waves the universe presents to us. Ride them until they dissipate. These momentous shifts are gifts. If you have trouble seeing the rhythms of your life, create your own. After all, that's why we are here, are we not? To create?

It's time to step into our role as creators and not pawns. The laws will operate regardless. We might as well use them to our advantage.

Create Your Own Rhythms

To create rhythm is easy. Just set up a plan and follow it consistently. It doesn't matter how messy it is at first, and trust me, it will be messy. Don't listen to your mind, don't listen to your friends, don't even listen to your mentors. Figure out what you want to do, make a plan of how it will be done, and repeat it daily.

Have you ever been inside a pool and made waves with a board? At first, all you do is splash around haphazardly. Pure chaos. But after a minute or so, you begin to find your rhythm and the waves come easily. The wave-making comes easier and the water begins to rock you just as much as you are rocking it.

This, my friends, is what we call momentum. You've created your own waves and are now basking in the ambience. Don't bask too long, however, for the waves and rhythm will only last a few moments. This is how we operate our lives. Create a rhythmic wave, and stay at it, so that we can ride our own self-perpetuated momentum.

These rhythms are found in something as simple as routine! Yes, you heard me right. Routine, be it daily, weekly, or monthly. The more often the better, however. These routines create the healthy kinds of swings in our realities. Instead of going day by day with our heads in the clouds, allowing the world to happen to us, we set up shop and create a foundation from which our lives can flow back and forth on the *frequency we desire.*

We can't stop the pendulum, but we can create our own pendulum and influence its swing. Think about it. Our world is dictated in part by our internal mechanisms, meaning our thoughts, perceptions, reactions to the world, and what we experience. If we set up a positive rhythm disguised as routine, we emanate *exactly* how we want our world to swing. All we have to do is hold on to that rhythm no matter how chaotic it gets in order to give the world a chance to dance to our song, just like the waves in the pool. It looks like chaos at first but becomes smooth after a while. Everything that stems from the routine should, in most cases, reflect that premise.

There's a catch, of course, just to keep us on our toes. After all, you didn't really think it would be that easy, did you? While observing that our experiences can be dictated by us creating and utilizing rhythm, we must not chastise or condemn experiences that we do not like. Some people get stuck in a victim mind-set and think bad things happen to them because the world is unfair.

Life is not unfair, nor is it fair. It just is. We demonstrate our free will in how we recode the universe as we would like it to be. All encounters have within them lessons, and I've come to find that the more ill-received an encounter is, the more I have to learn from it. Remember, polar opposites exist. There cannot be good without bad, no darkness without light or light without dark.

That we have differences in the world is attributed to the clear definitions for what *is*. In other words, the more we define something, the more we simultaneously define its opposite.

Think about arguing a point. When someone *defies* you, he or she is questioning your point of view. As a result, we must dig down and really define what we believe so we may express ourselves clearly and hopefully win the argument.

A good friend of mine often questions any random theory I come up with, and I appreciate it because he forces me to define that which I deem to be "true." Without that definition, my words would be hollow and wishy-washy, vague at best. Even the word *define* comes from "defy." We must be put to the test. We cannot have one without the other.

One of my favorite movies is *The Nightmare Before Christmas*. Jack, the protagonist of the movie, is king of Halloween Town, a town devoted solely to scare 365 days of the year. All they do is work on the magic of things that go bump in the night. It's a magical place where monsters and ghouls can exist in a shockingly inviting atmosphere. The watcher soon learns that there is something awry, however. Jack's beautiful soliloquy describes his angst as follows:

Yet year after year, it's the same routine,
And I grow so weary of the sound of screams.
And I, Jack, the Pumpkin King.
Have grown so tired of the same old thing.

Oh, somewhere deep inside of these bones
An emptiness began to grow.
There's something out there, far from my home,
A longing that I've never known.

What a beautiful depiction of rhythm, or in this case, a lack thereof. Long story short (spoiler alert), Jack stumbles his way into Christmas Town—Halloween Town's polar opposite—and finds absolute fascination.

Christmas Town transforms him. He's thrust upon the opposite end of worlds. He's slammed up against his polar opposite, the pendulum is finally able to swing to the opposite side, and rhythm is restored.

Soon after he uses, "Year after year, the same routine ... deep inside these bones, an emptiness begins to grow ... a longing I've never known."

Oh, how the lack of rhythm torments! Have you ever had the sensation of longing for something unknown? A lack of rhythm, maybe? Life was never meant to be the same experience over and over again. To eradicate sadness is to eradicate happiness, and to get rid of extreme agony is to get rid of extreme happiness.

After a close call with death, Jack returns to Halloween Town with more enthusiasm than ever. His eyes are lit up with a newfound evil that he uses to power the next year of scare.

Balance is restored.

Let Go of Perfection

Perfection doesn't need to be attained by humankind because it doesn't do us any good to strive for something that's stagnant. That's the catch with perfection. It's unchanging, for if you reach perfection within something, and then change one aspect of it, it's no longer perfect. Therefore, perfection must remain constant.

Nothing in our world acts this way, though, so why should we? As stated before, everything that emanates from The All comes within it a swaying, a to-and-fro motion. Anything left in the same place too long must collapse. Otherwise, drastic measures and massive amounts of wasted energy must be used to keep it from changing. And even then, the compensation within the release of energy when it finally does collapse can be catastrophic. So we do not aim to be perfect or in other words, *stagnant*.

We have a new goal: to be adaptable, elastic, and open to any changes in our environment and/or our mental states of mind. Most people's sadness and heartbreak come from a lack of ability to let go. They cling to life, to their hopes and dreams and their ideas of how the world should be.

They find themselves caught up with the idea of perfection and then let themselves become overwhelmed with grief when that image doesn't manifest.

If we hold a specific idea of perfection in our heads and we somehow manage to find it, we become filled with happiness. When that circumstance begins to change—and it will—what happens when we don't?

Your idea of a perfect relationship, job, home, wedding, dog, parking spot, you name it, will never turn out the way you imagine it in your mind. There will always be a slight variation. Something will go "wrong." Something will shift.

It might be cloudy on your wedding day, your lover might not be as tall as you wanted, your dog might bark a little too much, or your food may be a little too cold. The trick to maintain a healthy mind-set for life is to anticipate this. It's about realizing that you're killing yourself in your unrealistic pursuit of perfection. And the harder you hold onto it, the more it will kill you when it doesn't happen.

Of course, with all this said, I don't mean to strive for the life of a sloth and not aim for anything. All I mean to say is that we must be like the water that Bruce Lee so eloquently describes, no matter what situation we are placed in. We must be able to mold ourselves. We must learn a way to fit into anything, anywhere.

This is the life of the manifester, of the true master alchemist. It's about letting go of all desired outcomes because there is far too much room for change within any given desire. To be hooked on a *specific* way of success is to blind yourself out of the infinite amount of possibilities in which success may present itself outside of your construct.

The universe wants you to succeed, but with the interactions of all the other souls on the planet, plus the infinite amount of variations with everything else, we cannot possibly know what perfection even means when the time finally comes.

Things have to change because other things are always changing, and since all life is tied together in a spider web of existence, so too must our ideas of what we want be open to the possibility of a little tug here and there.

The bad news is that nothing will ever go *exactly* as you want it. The good news? It might be a thousand times better than ever you imagined.

Plot twist.

How do you even know that your idea of perfection is the best possible scenario for something to work out? We could be so caught up with the way we think something should be that we blow by all other opportunities for success that would be *far greater than anything we thought possible*.

Many times we fail where we wanted to succeed in life—the loss of a job promotion, a girlfriend, getting into a specific school, for example. These "failures," however, only opened doors to experiences that stirred in us a fire that burns until the day we die.

We are shaped and molded by the so-called bad just as much as we are by the so-called good. It isn't until we understand that and are open to the possibilities that come with that knowledge, that we can take full advantage of the variations of outcomes in our lives.

True creators, we become.

Do you think humans would have evolved had there been stagnancy in the evolutionary chain millions of years ago? The ability to change and adapt allowed plants to be able to chemically synthesize sunlight and make food, literally out of thin air.

It allows bacteria and fungi to constantly change and break down all the poisonous toxins we throw out into the earth.

If you want to find perfection in the world, find out all the ways it is not.

That's where the truly ground-shaking breakthroughs come from, whether it's from some new animal created or a dream job you didn't even know you wanted until the beautiful e-mail appeared on that random Tuesday morning.

There is a certain kind of beauty that we can tap into if we choose to rethink perfection. And it finds us when we see ourselves as being perfect even with our imperfections. Our quarks, when appreciated, can be used as something that sets us apart from the rest of the crowd.

All the blemishes, the silly nuances of our personalities, are what the world falls in love with. We all know that the objective, empirically stagnant perfections found in retouched photographs are not real—not in the sense that we can touch or feel, at least. What is real is what we come across every day. Change, imperfection. It is the way your messy hair looks in the morning or the way you stutter when you're nervous. Those are the things your lover will remember when you're miles away.

CHAPTER 7

The Law of Cause and Effect

*Shallow men believe in luck. Strong men believe in
Cause and Effect.*

—*Ralph Waldo Emerson*

THE LAW OF CAUSATION is the sixth hermetic law. It's simple, not
at all flashy, but there are parts in it that will shine plenty of light
on the darker parts of the universe. It can show you why it was
that the neighbor's dog pooped on your lawn, or it can describe
the fall of the Roman Empire. It's as simple or complex as you
need it to be. It all depends on your ability to dig deep, to expand
your consciousness. Remember, the world's most precious gems are
usually found buried deep within her surface. If you want to fish
out some substantial gems, you better dig deep.

At this point, that everything happens for a reason should be
known and understood. Looking back at all the various laws, we
are able to deduce that life is by no means random and left up to
chance. There is no such thing as dumb luck. The universe operates
within the mind of The All, and the Mind is intelligent. There is

structure and boundary. Everything in the universe is tied together. Chance is but a name for law not recognized. You must believe this concept in order to make any progress with the evolution of your consciousness.

First, there is no hope for those who don't believe everything in the universe is connected. Those who believe in blind luck create an existence where everything is out of their control. They are right, for our worlds are what we believe. Once these ideas spread and finagle their way into the mind, you will forever be changed.

As stated at the outset, once you start, it is best finished.

Let's begin with our perceptions of the world. If we are to study the mechanisms of life, we must look at the gears that drive those mechanisms. We are no longer at liberty to take things purely at face value. My god, what a wasteful world this would be if all we did was graze across the surface of things, never diving down into the depths of the ocean to learn the secrets of the waters.

Let's rid ourselves of the notion that there is an *absolute* cause to any particular situation. If everything is tied to everything else, there is no real cause so much as a wave in the ocean isn't the original wave. The science of oceanography shows us how wind energy drives waves. The energy, which was brought about by changes in atmospheric pressure, which was brought about by fluctuations in temperature on the earth's surface, which was brought about by a combination of global weather patterns, which was brought about by solar properties, which was brought about by the sun, all the way down to the original thought.

The creation of the universe, to the best of our knowledge, was the original cause from which every action takes place. Everything since then, and until the end of time, is just a constant evolution. It's a constant change representing the flow of original creation. In terms of the big bang, you and I *are* the big bang. We are still that original event continuing its way into the void.

Sometimes I get the notion that we are stagnant. I feel that we are at the top of the food chain and that where we are in the universe now is something that is a complete product of the original big bang. But I was wrong. The big bang didn't *happen*; the big bang *is happening*.

Imagine this. You put a piece of dynamite into a watermelon and set it off. What do you see? A blown-up watermelon. The explosion will send the watermelon in every direction as far as the energy will allow. This is our universe, expanding out into every direction. However, because the scale of our universe is shy on infinite, the relation of time passed and the scale of the explosion is incomprehensible to human minds. In other words, it looks like we are standing still.

What does that mean?

It means that we can slow down the explosion of the watermelon to one and one trillionth to the power of ten and see that the explosion isn't moving at all. But really, when viewed in real time relative to us, it's moving incredibly fast. That is where earth is, in an explosion so colossal it seems like it is not moving at all. We are just a fragment of exploded watermelon that hasn't even left the interior of the fruit yet, still awaiting its blast into the unknown.

This example is only a demonstration to show the continuity of life. It shows that it is much easier to make sense of things when we step back and look at the bigger picture, when we avoid losing ourselves to the moment. After all, you can only ever connect the dots when you are looking back. That's when we realize that life could not have happened any other way.

Saying that every effect has an original cause does not mean that everything that is done has a reason. It means that everything that ever *is*, period, has a reason *and* a direction. This is cause and effect.

What do I mean by that? I mean that we need to stop looking at why things are and start thinking about how things *will be*. It's beautiful. This is how we become creators. Of course, looking at the past shows us how the dots are connected, but if all we ever do is look at the past, we are as stagnant as those being moved instead of those who are moving.

This is the law of correspondence in action. If everything happens because of past events, everything that happens *must also influence future events*. Sages throughout history have told us to be weary of dwelling in the past. And they were right. The past does not exist anywhere but in our minds. Therefore we should not allow it to dictate our present.

Instead, let the present dictate the past, and also the future. Think of a boat riding through the ocean. The boat is us moving through time. The past is represented by the wake. The boat creates the wake, not the other way around.

Recognize that every single event that will ever happen to you will influence your life in some way or another. All thoughts, feelings, and emotions, all your happiness, sorrow, hopes, and dreams are being determined *from this very moment in time*. Unless you choose to be consciously aware of every moment in your life, things will continue to be dictated by forces outside of your control.

The Birth of Responsibility

We are no longer poor little creatures at the whim of circumstantial events with this knowledge of cause and effect. If we stay open and listen just a bit harder, we start to catch strange feelings. We start to glimpse into the seams of reality.

You are this universe. It is constantly creating and evolving, and therefore you too are constantly creating and evolving. Everything is happening and being done at exactly this moment. The universe was not created in the past. It was created now. If the universe was created in the past, at that point in time, it was still created now.

Its expansion and creation are still happening now, in the same way the wake of our ship creates here and now. This truth rattles many of those who buy heavily on the sorrows of their past. And it should. Certain truths can do that. As we look into our past traumas as a definition, it turns into a scapegoat. We end up trying to look off the back of the ship using a fading and distant wake as an explanation for how things are turning out now.

In Eckhart Tolle's book *The Power of Now,* he writes about how our past torments us. Our minds have shackled our souls and then cast them into dungeons created by itself. Things never happened to you in the past. They happened in the now. The only difference is that it was in a different space of awareness distorted by the illusion of continuity and time, which is good news, because it is still now.

Everything is happening now.

If an event influenced you by happening in some other "now," it can sure be influenced again in your current "now." This is why I say we are no longer creatures of circumstantial events. Not with this knowledge. We are only at the mercy of past events when we are not awakened to the truth. The truth that we can change exactly who we are at any point. The only place you can escape the now is in your mind, and the mind can be a foolish thing full of endless trickery.

Now, I'm not saying that you aren't hurt from what happened in the past. I'm not in any way trying to belittle or make insignificant any events that may have caused you pain. All I am trying to do is rid you of the poisonous reasoning your mind tries to create as a result of them. A mechanism in your mind is tied to the notion that you are who you are solely because of past events, but it's only because you believe them to be true that they "are." You have the ability to change. It took actions to make you who you are, which means there are actions that will change you into someone new if you choose to.

Remember when we said that nothing in this universe remains constant except The All itself? The second law of thermodynamics states that there is a natural tendency of any isolated system to degenerate into a more disordered state. If everything is energy, so are your inhibiting beliefs. Let them also degenerate. Do not believe that some events that happened in the fading wake of your life can hold you at knifepoint from change.

Everything is headed toward collapse, including your past. What happens to things in nature that impede the flow of change? In science, we see that everything eventually gives, whether a dam, a volcano, or an overloading population. Nature will always seek balance. If you refuse a change within yourself, then you too shall break.

Life is funny that way. All it wants to do is move, change, and evolve. It wants more complexity, more beauty.

But we refuse that change.

We don't want to accept that we can be different than we were yesterday and throw it all to fate. We throw it all to something outside of our hands. And then we cry "woe is me" until our last breath. And who knows? We might be right to think that. But do we want to be right if being right means we are truly helpless and can't do anything to change that?

If you are reading this book, is that the type of life you want to live? Or are you a treasure hunter—a truth-seeker tearing through the uncharted jungles of your psyche to learn and discover just how incredible and capable you really are?

People like you and I don't have time for naysayers, for those who hinder us and fill our hearts with doubt and perpetuate self-loathing and self-pity. Even if it means we die trying, at least we die with a smile on our faces. We will look at them and say, "I have lived. What have you done?"

Ah, the wonders of the universe! So often we think that laws limit and bind us, surely this one more than others, for doesn't it seem a bit hopeless that we cannot act outside the influence of some event? Laws, however, do not limit us at all. They simply show us the ways in which the world operates, and therefore how our lives must be operated. *As above, so below.*

It shows us processes so we may create with ease. These laws are simply blueprints for building. Life needs order in order to create itself. It needs a platform in which to obtain information on how to move forward. Without that information, nothing would be able to progress or solidify.

Laws are not meant to bind. They are blueprints for evolution. They are archetypes that allow us to grow into entities more powerful and advanced than our wildest imaginations. The only reason we become trapped is because our perception of law is skewed. Most people believe they are at the will of their heredity. They say things like, "I am a product of my environment," or "I am the way that I am because of my parents."

Let me ask you something. Who is the "I" that admits they are how they are because of their parents? And if those people are so aware that they know they are who they are because of their parents, why is it that they cannot be someone else because they know that?

In other words, once you know you are how you are because of a certain reason, the only reason you are *still* the way you are is by choice, not chance. I'll let you in on a secret I learned recently. Your habits are not at all habits. What you call a habit, I call a copout. Remember, we program our reality with our thoughts, words, and actions.

Let's begin the reprogramming process right now.

Most people will say that a habit is something we do not have control over. I call bullshit. Let's redefine the word *habit*, shall we? Let's call a habit something that we do regularly, that we do not know we are doing. The key thing to understand is that we are unaware of what we are doing. Everything we do knowingly, we do by choice.

Do you smoke? I'm sorry, but that's not a bad habit; it's a bad choice. Do you anger easily and often say things you don't mean? Do you have a tendency to bottle up your emotions and not say what you mean to say when you mean to say it, like me? Again, that is not a bad habit; it's a bad choice.

Do not let yourself become a slave to situations and circumstances. Remember, circumstances do not define who we are. It is our state of being that defines us. It seems counterintuitive to say that we define ourselves within each and every moment, especially since I just got done saying that everything has a cause and an effect.

Yes, absolutely, things from your past influence who you are today, as well as the patterns and habits that you have. Understanding the law of cause and effect is to see how things come about, and more importantly how to change them.

Remember that with our new definition of a habit, once we know we are doing something, it changes from habit to choice. A habit implies something happening outside your control. A choice is always under your control. Accept that, and your life will change. You will stop blaming all the "bad" things in your life on outside circumstances. You will take responsibility, which is only your ability to respond, back into your own hands. Yes, you will need to be a little more diligent about the way you live your life. You'll need a great deal more focus, concentration, and soul searching to determine what you want out of life.

You didn't think creating the life you wanted *exactly the way you wanted it* was going to be easy, did you?

It's an adventure, this life. Adventures are never sunshine and rainbows from start to finish. They get very dirty and scary at times. I'm not saying that you should blame yourself for everything because you're a total failure and it's all your fault. Not at all. I'm saying you should take responsibility for yourself because when you do, the power is back in your hands. You can't be in total control of your life *unless you are in total control of your life*. Once you take control of the bad, you allow yourself to take control of the good.

I keep reiterating the fact that you can't have your cake and eat it. Do you think the universe will allow you to take all the credit for your success but no credit for your failures? Do you think you can say it's because of your upbringing you failed but that it's because of you that you succeeded? No, it is because of you that you failed and because of you that you succeeded. You don't get to pick and choose when you want to be in control of your life. You're either 100 percent in, or you're 100 percent out. It's time we stop blaming other people for our failures and start to take credit for our successes.

This is a call to individual power. No longer can society and the media dictate our lives. No longer do we have to listen to tabloids or famous people tell us what happiness is or how to express our own version of love. What if there are an infinite amount of ways in which we can have romantic love, yet we never allow ourselves to explore them because they are not to be found within the mainstream norm?

I follow in the footsteps of the late mystic Terence Mckenna, when I say to hell with the media. *Create your own culture.* What if success is a twenty thousand–dollar income living in the woods? After all, success to a native just a few hundred years ago was a zero-dollar income but the chance to tell stories around a campfire every night. If you want to make millions of dollars, however, then do that! Who cares if people call you corrupt or power hungry? It's all about creating our own experiences in the world. It's about creating through the power of thought and action with love, compassion, and empathy. You do this with ultimate love for those around you, and more importantly, love for yourself. Just remember that love for yourself must start with taking control of how your life is operated.

We cannot defy the laws of the universe, but we can use one law against another. We raise our awareness, and therefore our consciousness, so we can operate above the planes of existence. This is how the philosopher's stone works when turning lead into gold—not in the literal sense but in the mind. We know now that every action has its cause and that every cause has its effect, and in no way can we escape that. You will always, in one way or another, have your life disrupted by what happens to you. This also means, however, that you can always disrupt life by the way you happen to it.

To be creators of life is to play the part of cause instead of effect. You will be one or the other. This you cannot avoid, and one would be foolish to try. Stay present and focused. Your focus is energy, and energy is always much stronger when concentrated. Add a small magnifying glass to sunlight in a warm a forest and the forest will go up in flames. Your mind is no different.

The first step in determining the standing of your life is to evaluate your decisions. Take into consideration why you do the things you do. Everything has its influence. Where are yours coming from? Are they serving you? Did you put them in place, or were they put in place by someone or something else?

The key here is to be unreasonable. Do not justify *anything*. The truth is, everyone is right in his or her own sense. Everyone has valid reasons as to why his or her life is in shambles or laced in gold. But that's not the point. The point is that you have certain goals, landmarks, and checkpoints you need to achieve in your life, and unless you change the mechanisms of your current situation, you will not have anything manifest that is different from the old. This brings me to my next point: do not believe that you can watch, do, or be involved in anything and it not have an effect on you.

Your mind is strong. I will not dive into the realm of things like the placebo effect, for you already know it to be true. But I will share this: it is scientifically proven that your mind cannot distinguish the difference between what is real and what isn't. Run, and a certain part of your brain will light up like the sky, but only *think* about running and the same part of the brain will ignite. This is how thoughts are able to create reality.

By constantly speaking in language that brings you closer to your goals, you are triggering responses in your subconscious mind *as if they were already true*. The universe only operates with what is, not what isn't. Studies on the ways your brain operates demonstrate that.

In the principle of polarity, we learned that the universe does not deal in what's "good" or "bad," for they are one and the same. It does not speak the language of "try" and "hope." It only speaks of what is. For this very reason, it is incredibly important to be conscious of the ideas and "truths" that find their way into your mind.

Everything that appears in your life appears for a reason. People, situations, encounters, conversations, and thoughts—they are all indicators of an internal mechanism. They are effects from an internal cause that you are consciously or subconsciously creating. These are ways of determining internal perceptions. This is why it is detrimentally important to be aware of the people and places we surround ourselves with.

What type of encounters are you trying to facilitate? What type of relationships are you trying to build? For most of us, it is difficult to hold strong to our beliefs and goals when the outside world is constantly blasting us with contradictory beliefs and patterns creating a forced cognitive dissonance. The most fundamental existence comes from our internal world, but that does not mean the external can't play its own role.

The effect of placing yourself within the grasp of contradictory thoughts is to (at the very least) create a type of cognitive dissonance within your psyche. If you want to create a paradigm that portrays the world as abundant in love, compassion, and genuine generosity, yet you watch the daily news and volunteer yourself to useless gossip, where do you think you'll end up?

We all know the news portrays a world that consists of an incredible amount of hate, violence, and scarcity. It fuels fear and shows complete contrast to what you are trying to create. So why expose yourself to it? Studies show that your brain literally does not realize that what you are watching on the screen is not actually real. The same hormones are pumped into your body as if the event was actually happening right in front of you. This is why your heart rate increases when you watch a horror movie. Your mind thinks it's really under attack.

When using the principle of cause and effect, we know that *every* cause, say, circumstances you put yourself in, will have its effect on your internal world. There is no escape other than complete removal from that which you do not want and complete absorption into what you do want.

The cognitive dissonance created by subjugating ourselves to contradictory circumstances creates pure chaos. One side of your mind is fighting for a new way to broadcast, and the other is being attacked by every billboard, newspaper, and television show we come across. In order for the subconscious mind to attract like-minded circumstances, the broadcast must be strong, and it must be constant.

CHAPTER 8

The Law of Gender

Gender is in everything. Everything has its Masculine and Feminine Principles. Gender manifests on all planes.

—*The Kybalion*

THE LAW OF GENDER is the seventh and final law of the hermetic philosophy. We have reached it at last! And what a beautiful way to bring everything together, neat bowtie and all. Man and woman, masculine and feminine. We have everything we need to see the mechanisms of creation; everything in life is interrelated. Everything flows just as it should, in and out, up and down, light to dark, on every plane and within every facet of life—and as Pumba would say, "We burn like giant balls of gas burning billions of miles away."

The law of gender states that everything from the physical to the spiritual plane manifests within it both masculine and feminine properties, and it is from proper integration of the two genders that creation occurs. A union of masculine and feminine is the only way something may come to life.

This law, however, must not be confused with sex, not in the way we use it in our everyday lives. Sex as we know it is merely an organic manifestation of the law of gender at work—both the act of sex as well as distinguishing a man from a woman. It is much more than that.

Everything in nature has in it both parts of gender, and we know this based on the principle of correspondence, as above so below. We have male and female animals and sometimes both in the same animal. In the plant kingdom, flowers have both stamen and stigma (male and female parts) in order to reproduce.

But gender doesn't only show as physical properties for creating through reproduction. Looking past the physical world and into the mental, we see that us humans can portray feminine mental states as well as masculine mental states within the same person, both needing their own necessary times for use and dedication (this we will touch on in a bit).

Creating, producing, generating: these are priorities of the principle of gender, no more, no less. Think of the law of gender as yin and yang. It can be seen as two poles of the same thing, only this time instead of simply demonstrating duality, we are trying to join two opposite sides to meet together to form something new.

Imagine positive and negative charges, only let's change the words a bit. Let's not use "positive" and "negative," for there is absolutely nothing wrong with either side of this pole to be called negative. Instead we will take science's side and use anode and cathode. Anode is masculine and cathode is feminine.

In science, cathode is merely the origin, the source of energy; it is like the womb of nature, birthing new life after the introduction of its male counterpart. If the vacuum of space, which holds the entirety of the universe, is the origin (the feminine), then the pervasion of consciousness (its counterpart, masculine) is what breathes life into the spheres of existence so that reality may take form.

Even the very foundation of physics shows how creation takes place by the attraction of the "positive" to "negative." Put simply, atoms are merely masses of negatively charged ions gathered around a cluster of positively charged ions. Beautiful.

The fundamentals of life are portrayed scientifically through the intricacies of the principle of gender. It's a win-win situation for the post–new age spiritual adventurer.

Blow up to a larger scale: the brain. What do we see? Well, there are two sides to the brain, right? A left hemisphere and a right hemisphere. Would it surprise you if I told you that each side of the brain had its own characteristics relative to the law of gender?

Everything is connected, remember! *As above, so below!* Never forget that. Mental gender shows how our minds are separated with both genders.

For example, our left hemisphere largely dictates the masculine affinities, also known as the intellect (logical, analytical, projected will, linear thought processes), while the right hemisphere is mostly designated for feminine aspects, which tie closely to our intuition (art, creativity, compassion, holistic approaches).

True success doesn't come from dominating any particular side. It comes from balance—a proper yin and yang approach to our approach to life. This balance we discussed in the chapter on rhythm involving polarity, timing, and swing. All these things we must utilize with the mind and with our cadences in life so that both sides work together, symbiotically.

Now that we see everything in life *must* incorporate both sides of gender in order to maintain proper healthy creation, we can realize the necessity for conscious thought processes involving both sides of the brain.

In other words, utilize both the feminine and masculine aspects of your mind *and* your actions and you will be able to accomplish anything.

How? Well, first we must see the purpose of these areas and how they conduct themselves. The feminine, which we learn from the behavior of electricity, female reproductive cycles, etc., is the origin of substance, which we can relate in this case to things like the imagination, thoughts, ideas, and concepts.

Sorry, men, but the feminine gender is far more active than the masculine—*far more.* This is my own conclusion, but just hear me out.

It is responsible for more activity on every plane and generally only needs one input for the creation process to begin, which it can finish very efficiently on its own, if you don't mind. Don't believe me? All right—on the physical plane, an apple tree only needs *one* microscopic grain of pollen (masculine) to fertilize its flower (feminine). The flower falls and grows an entire fruit from the single grain of pollen. The pollen grain turns to a fruit infinitely larger than its origin.

Still don't believe me? All right. Onto the mental plane. My projected will and analytical thought processes (masculine) drove me to write a book; my imagination and creativity (feminine) has been weaving words and random, chaotic thought processes and ideas into something tangible thirty-three thousand words later.

You see? The masculine aspect of the mind is like a rider on top of an elephant, merely guiding, but the true work is coming from the elephant (men, please do not use this analogy with a woman and call her an elephant). However, the two must be present for meaningful creation. And the feminine aspect must always be open to receive the masculine input.

Because of this, it is passive, it is prone to receiving, and we see this on the physical plane. Women (feminine) have a vagina, which receives an impulse (penis and/or sperm) and then creates and births new human life.

The masculine is, well, the opposite. It drives a pulse; it gives out; it expresses. It is the consciousness that fills the void of existence providing the fabric of the universe with information—something to work with. Masculinity is action and a little more thrusting.

The Deception of New Age Spiritualism

Here's where I am going to upset a lot of you, and you will have to forgive me, but it is necessary.

With today's New Age revolution has come a great deal of misconceptions about the operations and mechanics of the universe. One of them was already introduced in the beginning of this book where we saw that us humans are in fact not God himself. We are mental projections of "it," containing remnants of the creator by mere osmosis, for we saw in the principle of cause and effect that there can be no effect without containing within it a piece of the cause.

We are as Hamlet in the mind of Shakespeare, not the other way around. But there is another great tragedy in today's scope of spirituality. It is the idea that we must be completely passive about the conditions of the world and the things that go on in it. But we cannot merely go with the flow of life like a leaf floating downstream. The idea that no matter what happens, blind faith and trust in the good of the world will bring about the change that we seek will not work.

Yes, we talk about our state of being defining circumstances, but that does not mean the outside world does not exist impartial to us. We are co-creators living in a world that is ours to share, and we must not close our eyes to atrocities that are real. We have to be careful not to be blinded by concepts, saying we only pray and meditate on things.

Remember that life requires balance. Life requires a certain rhythm and cadence for proper manifestation, and without this balance, everything collapses. The law of rhythm states that everything swings from one side of the pendulum to the other. It's what balances life and brings about definition to processes. What we have today, though, does not represent this swing.

We have instead embraced a complete and total feminine perspective, relying solely on passivity and intuition and very little action. The law of attraction and its popularity emphasized that we only need to think things into existence. We are taught by most spiritual fanatics today that passiveness and "allowing the universe to move as it will" are the way to enlightenment, but unfortunately, it is not that easy.

Passivity is only one side of the spectrum, and to ignore the other side is to ignore another side of existence and of the operating systems of The All, which is like perpetually taking one step forward and one step back, never gaining any real ground.

We see in today's world a society torn apart by ignorance and nescience, but knowledge will free us all, and it has never been more available than it is today. This means we have no one to blame but ourselves for the troubles we see around us. We have dominating governments bent on control through brutal force.

The world is out of balance. It is dominated by masculinity, and of course, it would make sense to turn to the opposite side in order to fix the problem, which is why we see a turn to the feminine in the new age culture.

We see philosophies on the rise that preach passiveness and a destruction of the ego along with its masculine tendencies in order to bring more compassion into the world. This is a turn in the right direction, of course, but still an imbalance. We end up with a society on one extreme or the other.

Life is about balance; it is about yin and yang, a symmetry between the genders, not a total absorption with one or the other. The feminine will receive information from the masculine, always. It *must* have an input in order to complete the whole—to generate the new, whether it be on the physical plane, the spiritual plane, or anything in between. There is no way around it.

The feminine will always be receiving impulses, and those impulses with be laden with information. It will process *only with that information*, for there cannot be an effect which within it does not lie a piece of the cause. What goes in must come out. This is why we must not give in too heavily to mainstream new age practices and philosophies.

Most of today teaches that we must allow the occurrences of life to happen. This is receiving an impulse. If we only ever receive impulses, then we become gullible. We believe anything and everything. Instead of dictating, we are dictated. Instead of generating, we are generated. We remain the effect and not the cause.

We can't let our world be run into the ground and led by those who would see us serve instead of lead. We cannot only sit in our rooms and meditate and pray; we must also take action. We must embrace both aspects of ourselves for creation to commence. One does not rise to power over themselves and their goals by fairy-tale actions, by sitting, waiting, and wishing. It requires a pulse; it requires action.

I'll teach you how to use the principle of gender to overcome obstacles and consciously create harmoniously with our own proper intentions, taking the rest of humanity in mind as well.

Action is required for meaningful change. It is the other aspect of gender that sparks and completes creation. A flower must be pollinated by its male counterpart in order to seed and reproduce;

so must our lives be pollinated with our masculine counterparts. This is like the breath of consciousness. The principle of gender is all about creation and regeneration, and it may only occur when both sides are brought together.

Using all the principles in this book, we now have enough knowledge to understand whether something is whole and in line with the natural laws of the world. This book was never about answers. It has always been about tools. We now have all the tools necessary to create wholeness in any event or circumstance. We are now armed for proper identification of patterns, for that is part of why we are here—to witness patterns and learn from them. Then we make our own patterns using law. Take a look at this passage:

Be formless. Shapeless. Like water. You put water into a cup, it becomes the cup. You put water into a teapot, it becomes the teapot. Water can flow, or it can crash. Be water, my friend.

It was written by one of the greatest martial artists to have ever lived, Bruce Lee. This is a perfect depiction of what a balanced energy is capable of. Water, like the mind, takes on both gender counterparts. It is passive enough to take on any form. It is limitless. It is soft and malleable enough to be anything and everything, flowing down a mountainside, choosing the path of least resistance every time as it cascades down with complete ease.

But at the same time, it is active and can crash down gullies and tear valleys thousands of miles long and thousands of feet deep. It can gouge caverns under mountainsides, revealing gem-like insides big enough to fit buildings in. Water integrates both masculine and feminine properties and therefore is nearly unstoppable.

The feminine is incomplete without the masculine and the masculine incomplete without the feminine. Alone, the masculine acts hastily. It moves without restraint, order, or reason. It lacks thoughts of anything outside itself, and compassion dwindles; chaos follows a society dominated from the masculine.

The feminine, on the other hand, is prone to constant reflection, far too much energy in the introspective, which leads to a lack of movement, stagnation, and ultimately a sacrifice of control to outside influences. This sacrifice of control comes from the input constantly coming from outside agendas and not its own.

Hark! Half-truths are the most dangerous lies. There is nothing more misleading than having only one part of the natural law at your side, never seeking anything new because of the seemingly wholesome piece of knowledge one might *think* they contain.

But there is beauty in the world. No matter what your peril may be, it too will pass. And maybe that is why the world is beautiful, because nothing ever lasts, not even death. There is something moving and detrimentally melancholy about something that will not be around forever, ever changing and evolving.

After all, what would the beauty be in something that lasted forever? There would be nothing special about it, no novelties or innovation or a sense of uniqueness. Happiness swings to sadness, old to new and new to old. It gives us a chance to experience the infiniteness of existence with a fresh start each and every time, ever growing toward source and oneness. See the patterns of the world. See the patterns of yourself, and realize that you are the light you seek, and always remember, we are all in this together.

This is the end of what I can offer you. Now make it your beginning.

Printed in the United States
By Bookmasters